KIDS IN THE KITCHEN

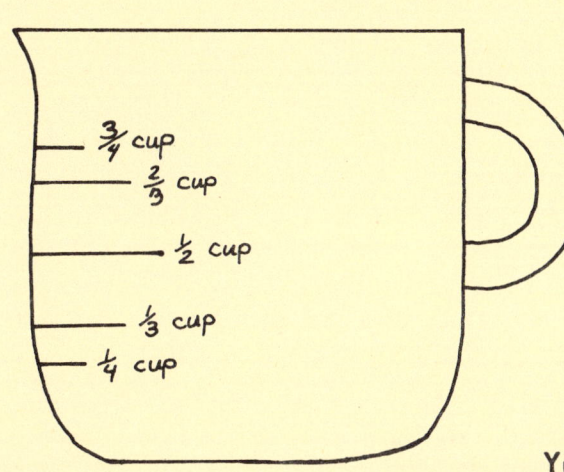

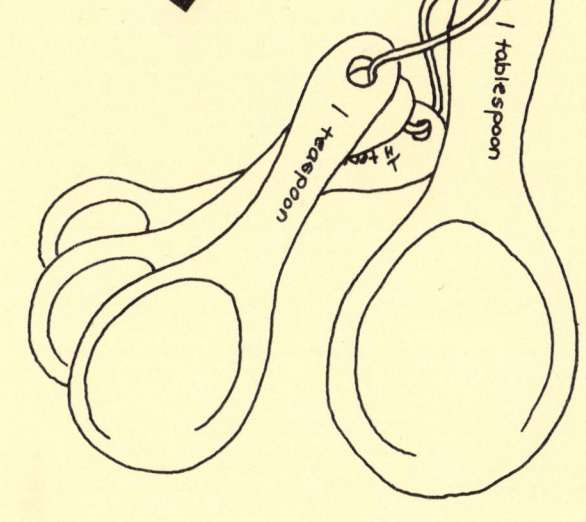

Yummy Recipes.
Nutritious, Fun Foods for Home and School.
Specially Designed for YOUNG COOKS.

Developed and Compiled by
Nellie Edge

Lettered and Illustrated by
Pierr M. Leitz

© Copyright 1975 by Nellie Edge and Pierr M. Leitz. All rights reserved. No part of this book may be reproduced in any form by any means without permission in writing from the author and illustrator.
(Formerly published under title "Kindergarten Cooks")

Library of Congress Catalog Number: 76-48558
International Standard Book Number: 0-918146-18-6

PUBLISHED BY PENINSULA PUBLISHING, INC.

P. O. BOX 412
PORT ANGELES, WA 98362

Table of Contents

Introduction 1

No Bake Goodies 2
    Cookies
    Popcorn Treats
    Candy

Baked Products 45
    Cookies
    Icings
    Breads
    Pizza
    Pie

Fruits and Vegetables 101
    Salads
    Apples
    Jello
    Beverages
    Jelly
    Pumpkins
    Sprouts
    Soups

Other Fun Foods 146
    Playdough
    Fondue
    Peanut Butter
    Butter
    Ice Cream
    Fun With Food

Index 165

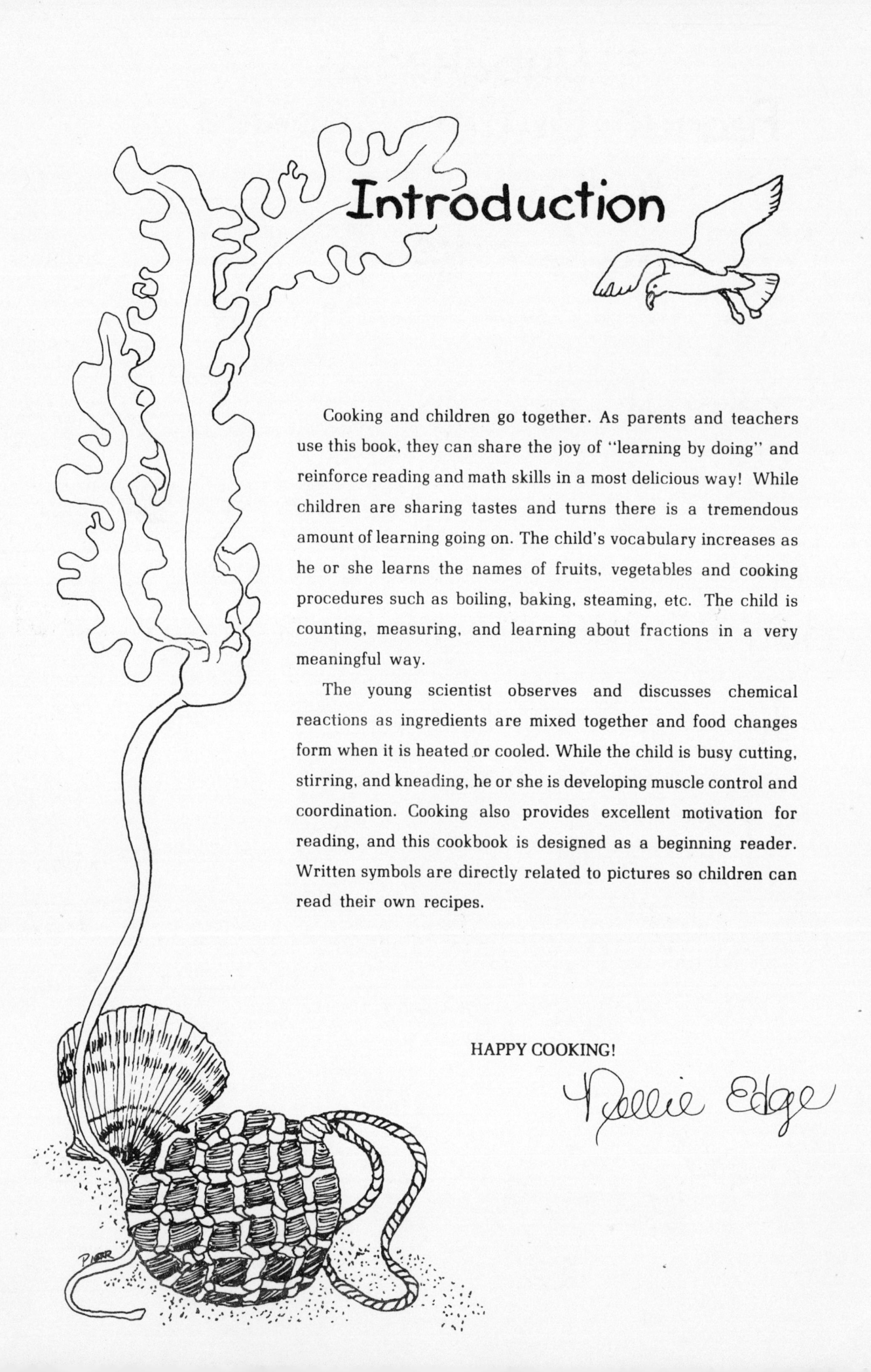

Introduction

Cooking and children go together. As parents and teachers use this book, they can share the joy of "learning by doing" and reinforce reading and math skills in a most delicious way! While children are sharing tastes and turns there is a tremendous amount of learning going on. The child's vocabulary increases as he or she learns the names of fruits, vegetables and cooking procedures such as boiling, baking, steaming, etc. The child is counting, measuring, and learning about fractions in a very meaningful way.

The young scientist observes and discusses chemical reactions as ingredients are mixed together and food changes form when it is heated or cooled. While the child is busy cutting, stirring, and kneading, he or she is developing muscle control and coordination. Cooking also provides excellent motivation for reading, and this cookbook is designed as a beginning reader. Written symbols are directly related to pictures so children can read their own recipes.

HAPPY COOKING!

Nellie Edge

Unbaked Peanut Butter Cookies

1 cup sugar
1 cup white corn syrup
2 cups peanut butter
4 cups Special K cereal

Combine sugar and syrup.
Boil for one minute.

Add peanut butter.

Add cereal. Mix well.

Drop from a teaspoon onto waxed paper.

Butterscotch Crunchies

1 package butterscotch bits
¼ cup crunchy peanut butter
3½ cups corn flakes

Melt butterscotch bits and peanut butter over low heat in heavy sauce pan.

Stir in corn flakes.

Mix well.

Drop from spoon onto waxed paper.

Fried Cookies

3 Tablespoons soft butter
½ cup brown sugar
1 cup white flour
2 Tablespoons powdered milk
1 teaspoon baking powder
1 teaspoon cinnamon
¼ teaspoon salt
½ cup wheat germ
3 Tablespoons honey
½ cup raisins
½ cup sunflower seeds
1 egg

Mix sugar and butter together in a large bowl.

Fried Cookies cont'd.

Sift flour, powdered milk, baking powder, cinnamon, and salt into the bowl.

Mix well.

Then add wheat germ, egg, honey, raisins, and sunflower seeds.

Mix together with your hands.

Shape dough into little balls, using flour on your hands and on the table.

Fried Cookies cont'd.

Roll balls in flour.

Flatten each ball.

Melt one tablespoon butter in electric fry pan at 300°.

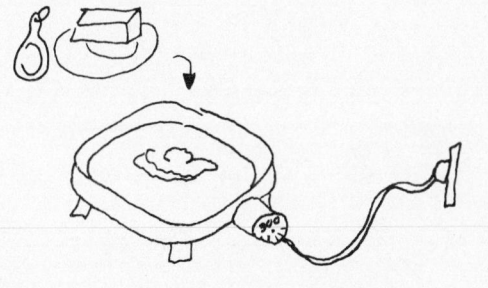

Fry cookies until golden brown on one side (about 5 minutes).

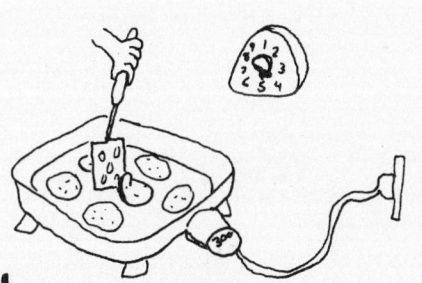

Then turn them over and fry about 2 minutes on the other side.

Remove cookies from pan. Let them cool.

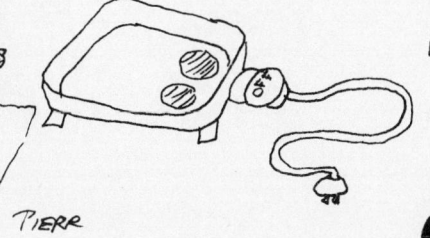

Fudge Cookies

2 cups sugar
3-4 Tablespoons cocoa
1 stick butter
½ cup milk

Mix these together.

Bring to a boil.

Let simmer for a few minutes.
Then add:

5 cups quick oats
½ cup peanut butter
1 teaspoon vanilla
dash of salt

Fudge Cookies cont'd.

Mix well.

Then cool.

Drop by teaspoonfuls onto greased pan.

8

Graham Cracker No-Bake Cookies

1 cup raisins
1 cup chopped dates
¼ cup honey
10 graham crackers

Pour raisins, dates, and honey into a mixing bowl.

Place graham crackers in a plastic bag.

Crush these with a rolling pin.

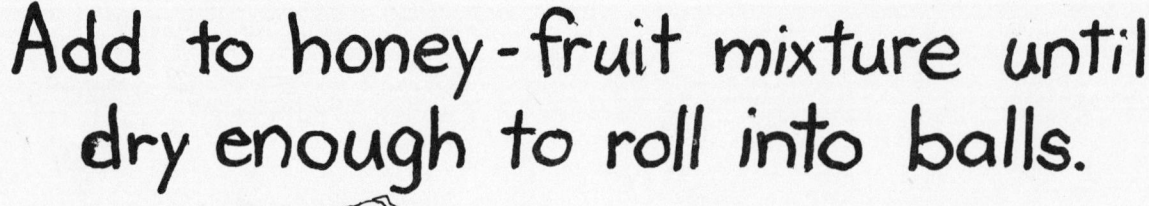

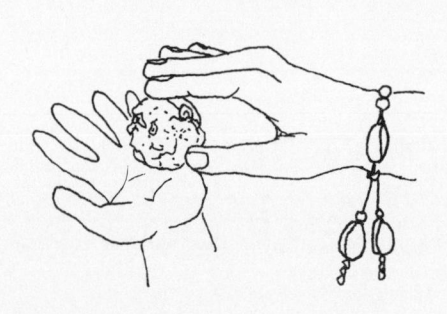

Add to honey-fruit mixture until dry enough to roll into balls.

No Bake Cookies

2 cups sugar
1 cube butter
3 Tablespoons cocoa
½ cup milk
½ cup peanut butter
3 cups oatmeal
1 teaspoon vanilla

Blend sugar and cocoa.

Add butter and milk.

Boil for 2 minutes.

Add peanut butter, oatmeal, and vanilla. Stir.

Drop from a teaspoon onto waxed paper.
Let cool.

Metric Peanut Butter Balls

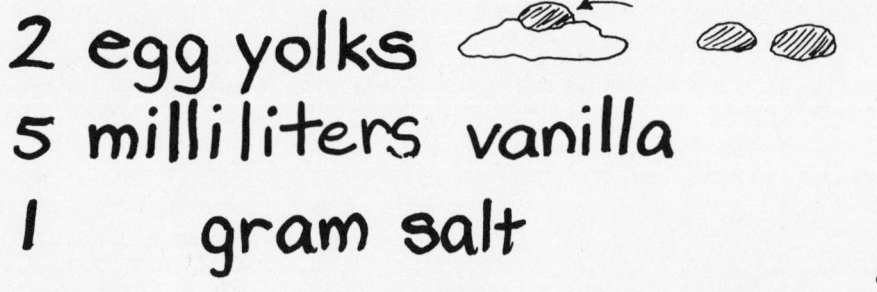

2 egg yolks
5 milliliters vanilla
1 gram salt
235 grams crunchy peanut butter
140 grams powdered milk
250 grams powdered sugar

Beat egg yolks, vanilla, and salt.

Add peanut butter, powdered milk, and powdered sugar. Mix well.

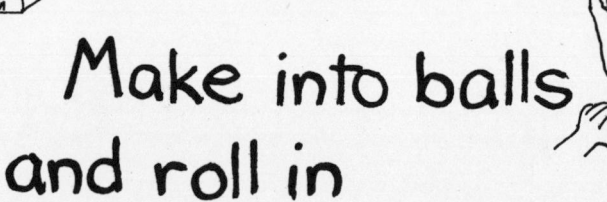

Make into balls and roll in remaining sugar.

Easy Walnut Panocha

1 cup brown sugar
2 cups powdered sugar
1/2 cup margarine
1/4 cup milk
1 cup broken walnuts

Melt butter and brown sugar
   in a sauce pan over
   low heat.
Add the milk.
Cook until boiling.

Cool.
Beat in powdered sugar
   until candy is thick.
Add nuts

Pour into a buttered pan.

Sesame Seed Honey Balls

¼ cup butter
½ cup sesame seeds
1 cup grated coconut
½ teaspoon vanilla
¼ cup honey

Melt butter in electric fry pan over low heat.

Stir in sesame seeds and coconut.

Stir the mixture over low heat for 5 minutes.

Turn off heat and add vanilla and honey.

Sesame Seed Honey Balls cont'd.

Put the candy in the refrigerator for one hour.

When it is chilled, roll into balls.

Keep candy refrigerated.

Makes about 3 dozen (36).

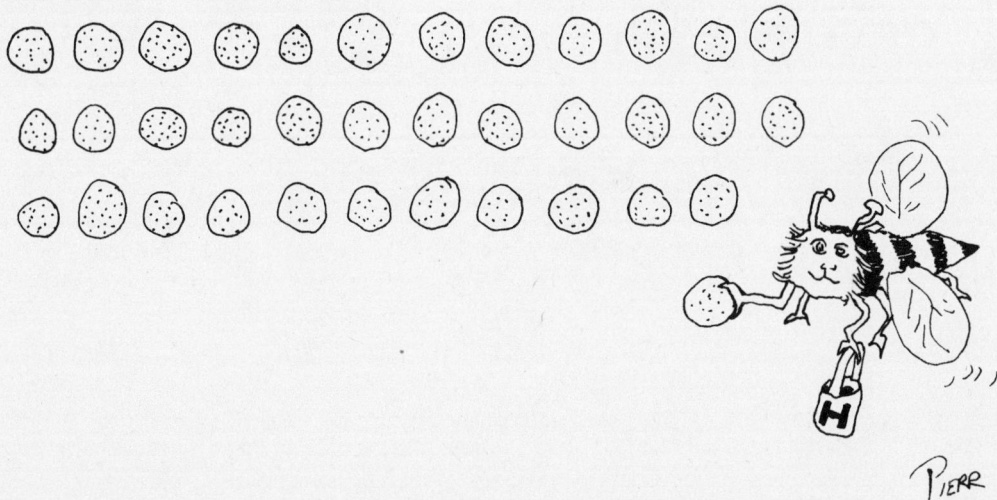

Rice Krispies Bars

¼ cup margarine
4 cups miniature marshmallows

½ teaspoon vanilla
5 cups Rice Krispies cereal

Heat margarine and marshmallows in a saucepan until thick and syrupy.

Add vanilla.
Pour over cereal.

Press into a greased pan.

Fa Shang Bo
A Recipe from China

1 cup sesame seeds
1 cup brown sugar
1 cup maple syrup
1 cup peanuts
4 cups puffed rice cereal

Mix sugar and syrup in a large, heavy pot.

Cook over low heat until mixture thickens — (5-8 minutes)

Stir often.

Mix in sesame seeds, peanuts, and puffed rice.

Pour mixture into buttered pan and press even with a spatula.

Chocolate Yummies

1 (6 ounce) package chocolate bits
1/3 cup margarine
16 large marshmallows
1/2 teaspoon vanilla
1 cup shredded coconut
2 cups rolled oats

Melt chocolate, margarine, and marshmallows.

Stir until smooth.

Remove from heat.

Add vanilla.

"Wait up!"

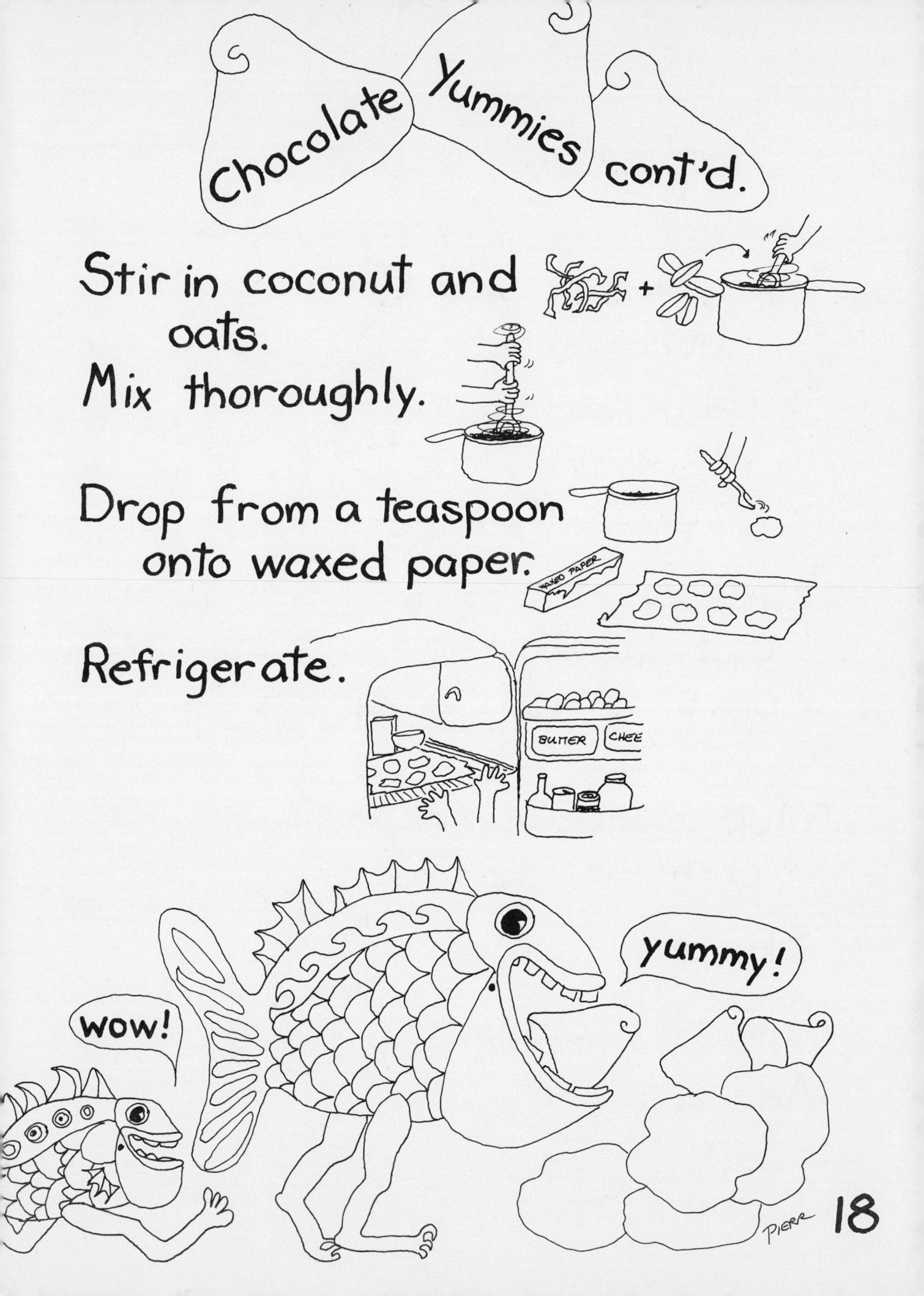

Chocolate Yummies cont'd.

Stir in coconut and oats.

Mix thoroughly.

Drop from a teaspoon onto waxed paper.

Refrigerate.

wow!

yummy!

Chewy Yum Yums

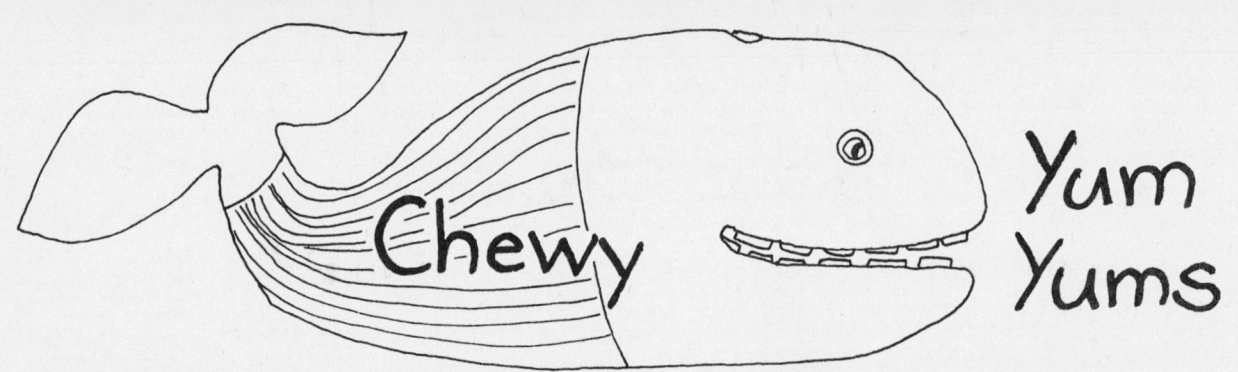

1 cup chopped nuts
1 cup chopped dates
½ package miniature marshmallows
24 crushed graham crackers

1 can Eagle Brand Milk

Mix all ingredients together in large bowl.

Make into balls.

Roll in fine coconut.

Corn Flake Balls

1 cup honey
1½ cups dried milk powder
1 cup peanut butter
1½ cups wheat germ
1 teaspoon nutmeg

crushed corn flakes

Combine all ingredients.

Shape into small balls.

Roll balls in crushed corn flakes.

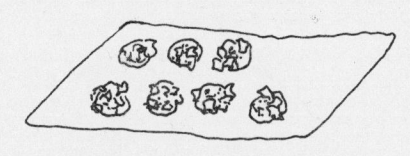

20

Peanut Yummies

1 cup sugar
¼ cup butter or margarine
⅓ cup evaporated milk
¼ cup chunky peanut butter
½ teaspoon vanilla
1 cup rolled oats
½ cup Spanish peanuts

Mix sugar, butter, and milk in a saucepan.

Bring to rolling boil.

Boil 3 minutes, stirring often.
Remove from heat.

Stir in peanut butter and vanilla.

Peanut Yummies cont'd

Fold in oats and peanuts.

Drop from a Tablespoon onto waxed paper.

Let stand until set.

Molasses Cheerios Balls

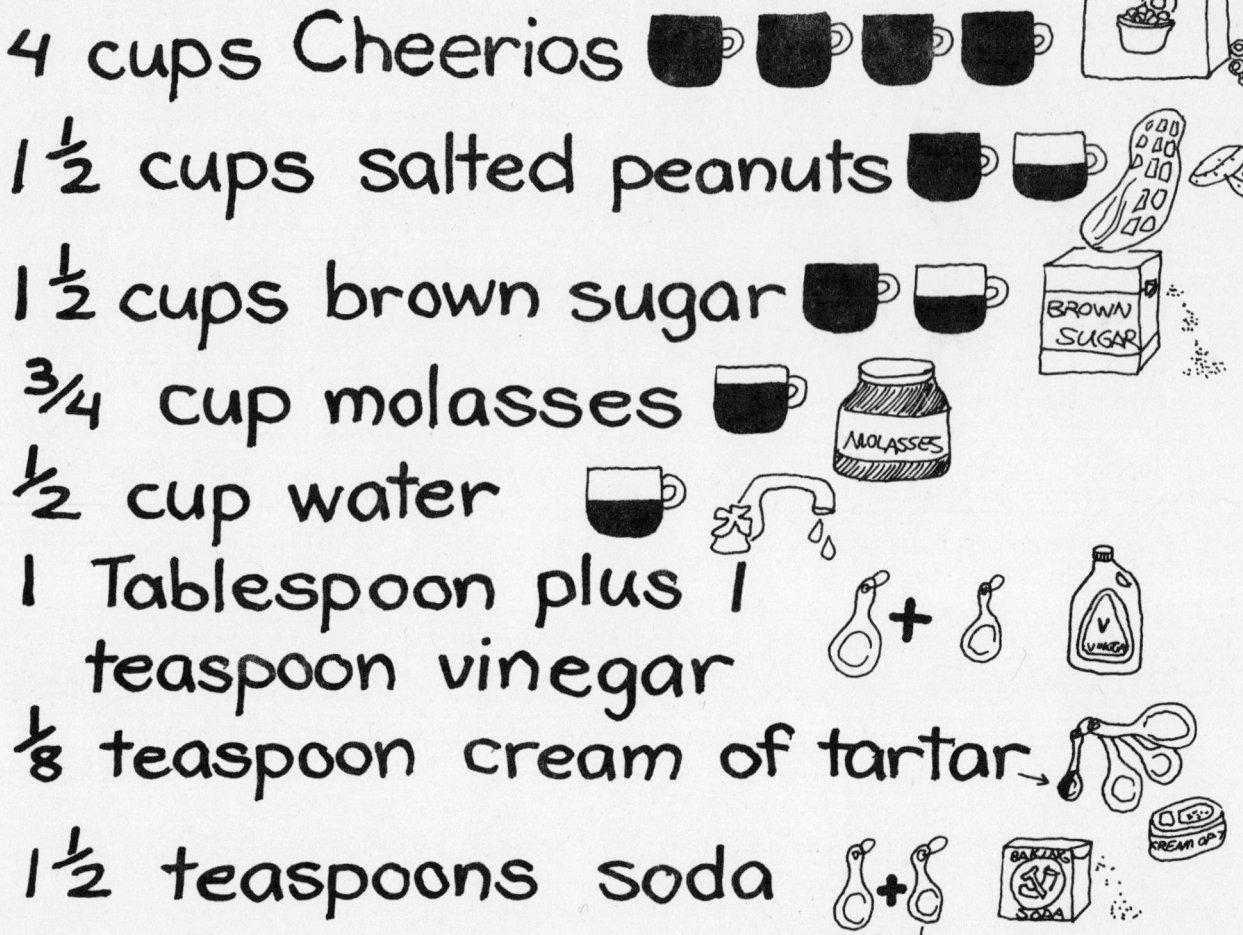

4 cups Cheerios

1½ cups salted peanuts

1½ cups brown sugar

¾ cup molasses

½ cup water

1 Tablespoon plus 1 teaspoon vinegar

⅛ teaspoon cream of tartar

1½ teaspoons soda

Mix Cheerios and peanuts into large greased bowl.

Mix sugar, molasses, water, vinegar, and cream of tartar in saucepan.

Molasses Cheerios Balls cont'd.

Cook over low heat, stirring occasionally, until a small amount of syrup forms a hard ball when dropped into water. (Hard Ball Stage)

Remove from heat.

Blend in soda and pour syrup over Cheerios-peanut mixture.

Mix well with greased spoon.

Allow to cool slightly.

Grease your hands and form mixture into balls.

Cool on waxed paper.

Makes 2 dozen (24) 2 inch balls.

Butterscotch Flings

¼ cup margarine
1 6-ounce package butterscotch bits
1 can chow mein noodles
1 package miniature marshmallows
¼ cup crunchy peanut butter

Mix peanut butter, margarine, butterscotch bits, and marshmallows in a sauce pan.

Melt on low heat, stirring until well-blended.

Butterscotch Flings cont'd.

Pour over noodles on a cookie sheet.

Spread until well coated.

Cut up when cool.

26

Pop Corn

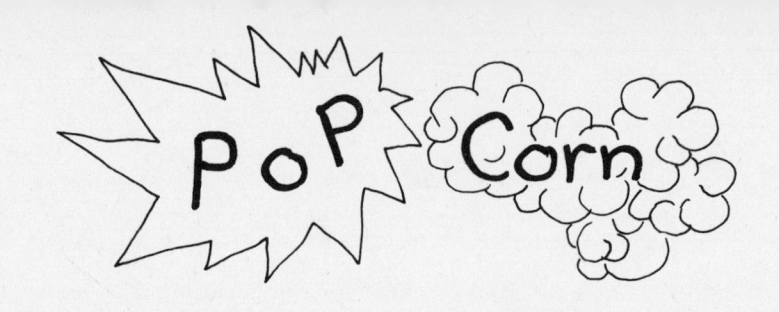

1 cup popcorn
½ cup oil

Pour popcorn and oil into popcorn popper.

Listen to the popping sound.

Watch the popping corn.

Give each child a single kernel of popcorn to examine.

Pour popped corn into paper cups. Add salt.

Count how many cups have been made.

Popcorn Cake

8 quarts yellow huskless popped popcorn

1 24-ounce package miniature marshmallows

1 stick margarine - melted

1 pound can salted cocktail peanuts

1 10-ounce package small gum drops

Pop the popcorn.

Dissolve marshmallows in the melted butter.

Combine popcorn, peanuts, and gum drops.

Popcorn Cake cont'd.

Add marshmallow mixture.

Mix well.

Press into a greased cake pan.

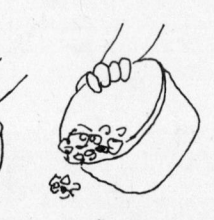

Cool until firm.

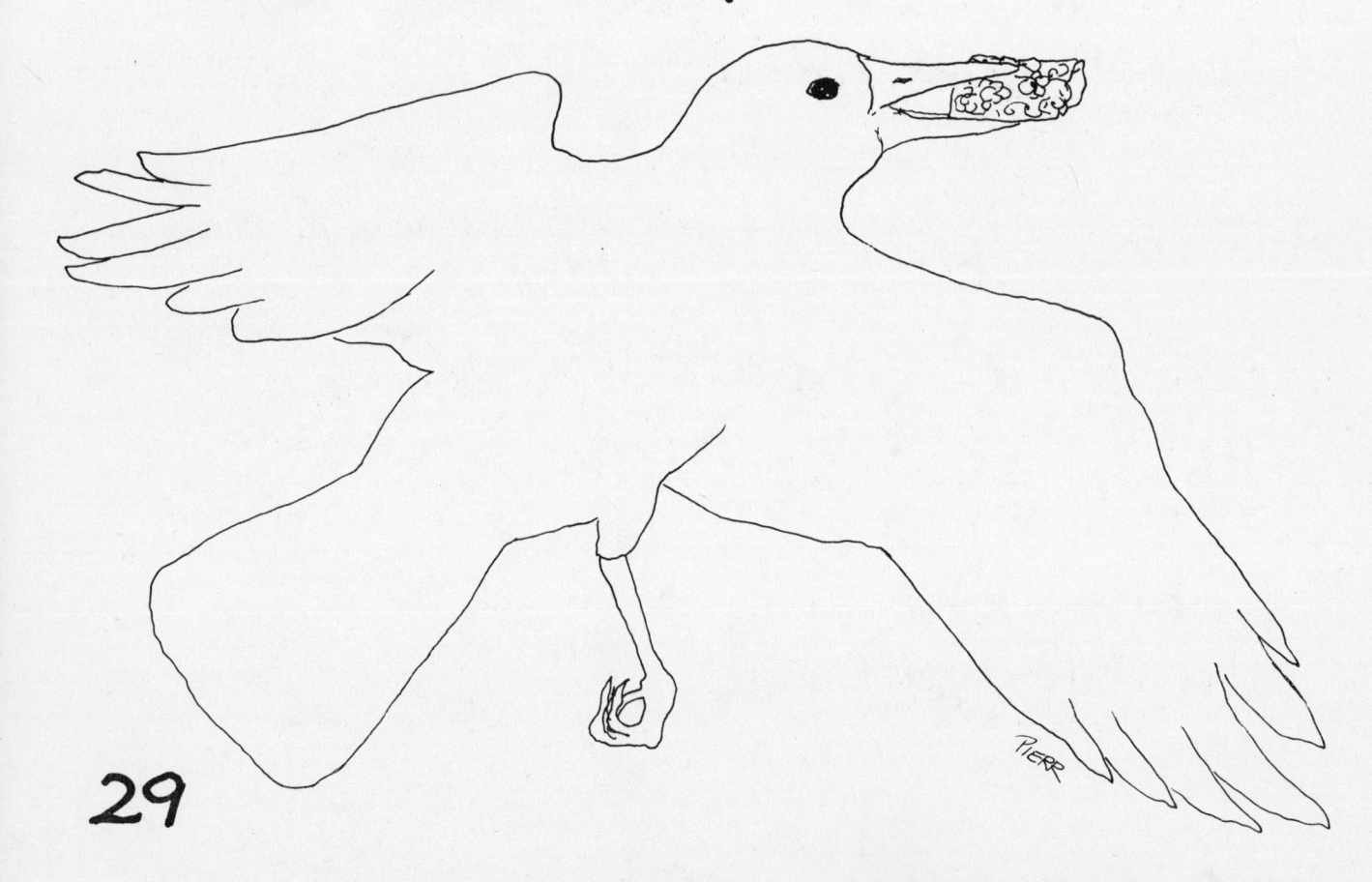

29

Helen's Popcorn Balls

4 quarts popped popcorn (16 cups)

3 cups Karo syrup

4 Tablespoons butter

Pop popcorn and measure it into large mixing bowl.

Pour syrup in pan and stir until it comes to a boil.

Continue stirring until it forms a hard ball in water.

Take off heat.

Helen's Popcorn Balls cont'd.

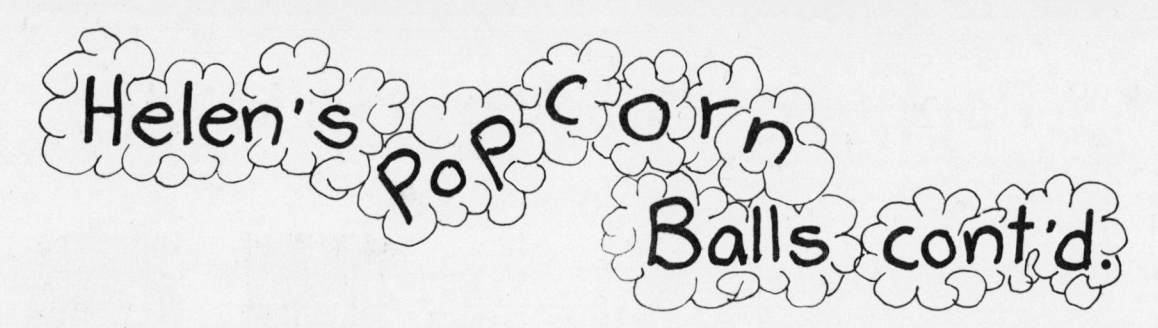

Mix margarine into syrup.

Pour over popcorn.

Butter hands and shape into balls, when syrup is cool.

Wrap individual popcorn balls in waxed paper.

Makes 12 large popcorn balls.

Honeyed Popcorn Balls

3 quarts popped corn (12 cups)

½ cup sugar

½ cup honey

1 teaspoon salt

2 Tablespoons margarine

1 teaspoon vanilla

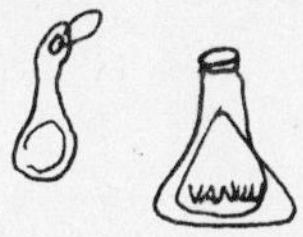

Pop corn and set aside in large bowl.

Combine sugar, honey, and salt in small saucepan.

Heat and stir to dissolve sugar.

Honeyed Popcorn Balls cont'd.

Boil to hard ball stage. (260°)

Add margarine and vanilla.

Pour syrup over popped corn and stir.

Butter your hands and shape into balls.

Wrap balls with waxed paper.

Cereal Candy

1 package butterscotch bits
½ cup peanut butter
3 cups Special K cereal

Heat butterscotch bits and peanut butter in a saucepan, until bits are melted.
Pour over Special K.
Mix well.
Drop from a teaspoon onto waxed paper.

Christmas Present Fudge

3 cups sugar
¾ cup margarine
½ can evaporated milk   (⅔ cup)
2 cups chocolate bits
1 jar marshmallow creme
1 cup chopped nuts
1 teaspoon vanilla

Combine sugar, margarine, and milk.

Bring to a rolling boil, stirring constantly.

Boil 5 minutes over medium heat, stirring constantly.

Remove from heat.

Christmas Present Fudge cont'd.

Stir in chocolate bits until melted.

Add marshmallow creme, nuts, and vanilla.

Beat until well blended.

Pour into a greased 13 x 9 - inch pan.

Let it cool.

Cut in squares.

Give away to friends!

Chocolate Candies

1 3-ounce package
   cream cheese 
1 teaspoon vanilla 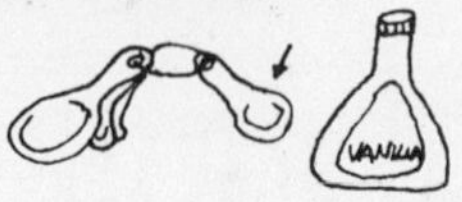
2 cups powdered sugar 
2 Tablespoons cocoa 
pecan halves

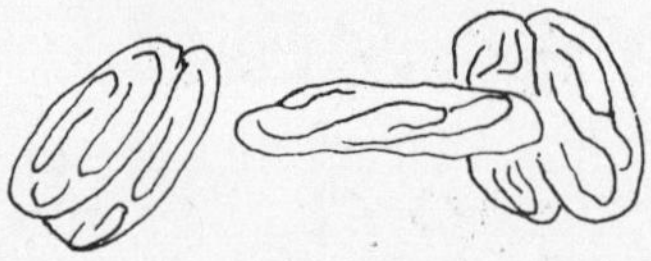

Beat cream cheese with vanilla.

Sift sugar and cocoa together.

Mix with cream cheese.

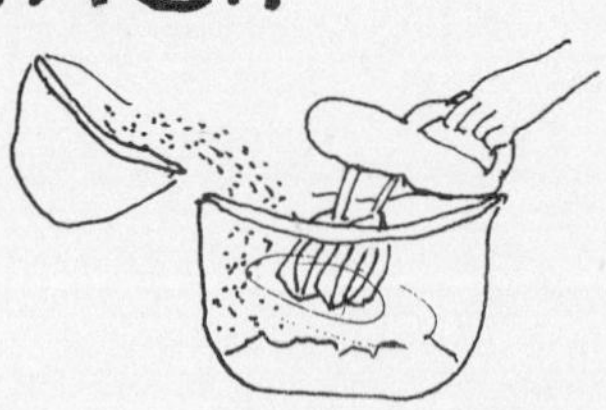

Drop from a teaspoon
   onto waxed paper.

Press a pecan half on
   each piece.

Yummies for Tummies

½ cup cocoa
1 cup honey
1 cup peanut butter
1 cup shredded coconut
1 cup raisins
1 cup sesame seeds
1 cup sunflower seeds

Mix and chill.

S'Mores

Milk chocolate candy bars
graham crackers
large marshmallows

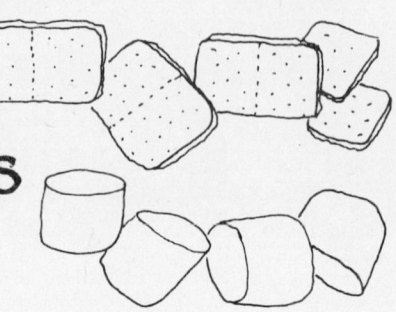

Place 4 squares of chocolate candy bar on graham cracker.

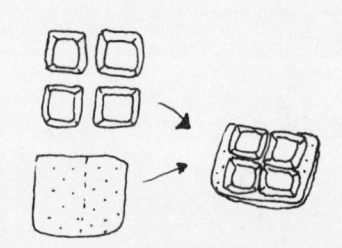

Toast marshmallows on a stick over a campfire.

Slip them onto the chocolate and top with second graham cracker.

Eat and then make S'more.

Umm-mm-good!

Caramel Stickies

¼ cup margarine

28 caramels

1 Tablespoon milk

¼ cup peanuts

4 cups cereal flakes (such as Product 19)

1 cup miniature marshmallows

Place margarine, milk, and caramels in large saucepan.

Cook over low heat, stirring often, until caramels are melted and mixture is smooth.

Caramel Stickies cont'd.

Remove from heat.
Stir in peanuts and
 cereal; mix until
 well coated.

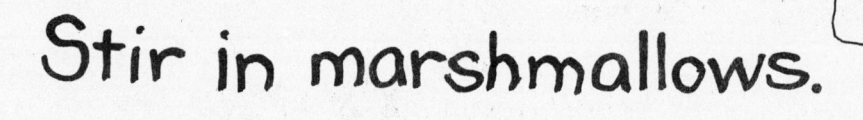

Stir in marshmallows.

Press mixture lightly into
 buttered 8 inch square pan.

Cool.

Cut into squares.

Molasses Taffy

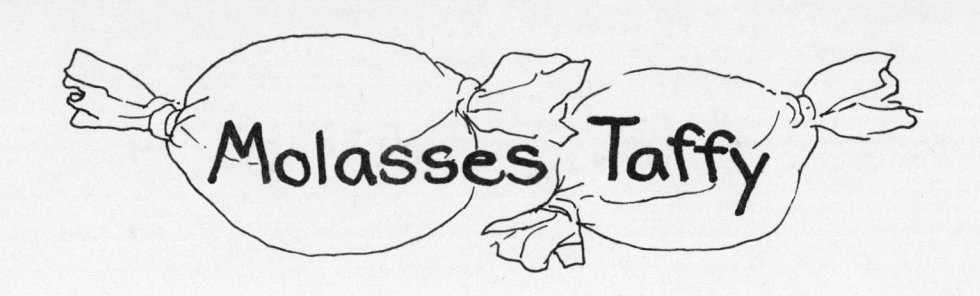

- 2 cups molasses 
- 1 cup sugar  
- 2 Tablespoons butter 
- 1 Tablespoon vinegar

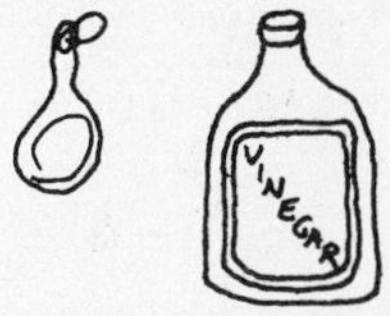

Combine ingredients in a heavy 3-quart saucepan.

Stir with wooden spoon until sugar dissolved.

Bring to boil over medium heat.

Continue cooking to hard ball stage. (260°)

Pour taffy into large buttered pan.

Molasses Taffy cont'd.

Turn edges of taffy to center of pan. with a spatula.

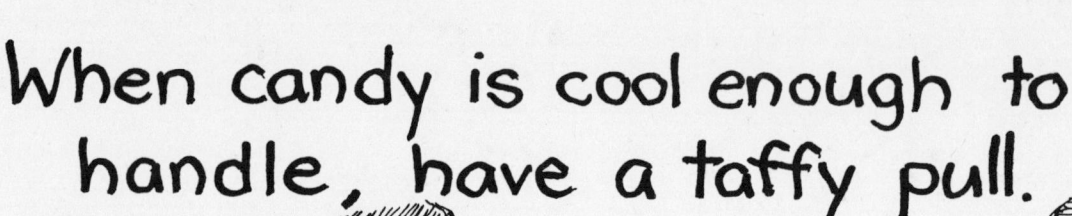

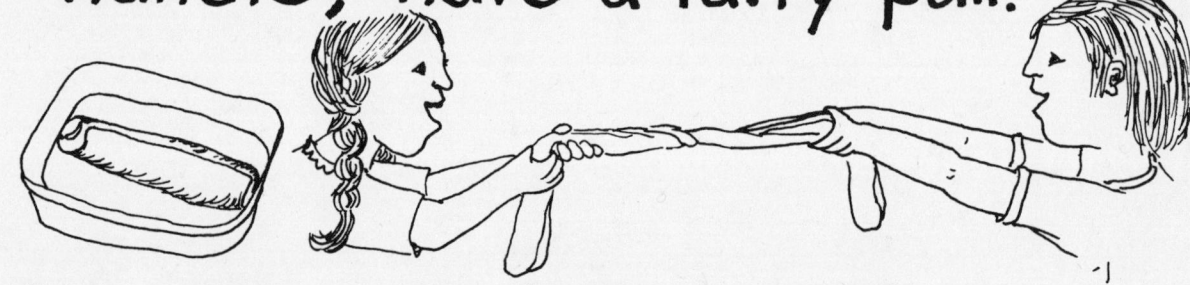

When candy is cool enough to handle, have a taffy pull.

Cut taffy into bite-sized pieces with buttered scissors.

Cool and wrap individual pieces in waxed paper.

Store in covered container.

Variation — Try adding 4 drops oil of peppermint before you pull taffy.

Creamy Cheese Mints

6 ounces cream cheese
1½ boxes powdered sugar 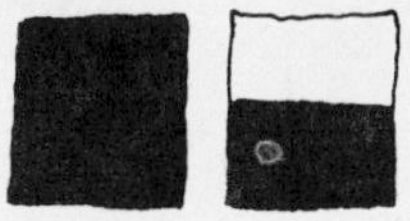 
food coloring 
¼ teaspoon oil of peppermint

Combine all ingredients in a large bowl until mixture is smooth and creamy.

(Add desired food coloring here)

Roll dough into balls.

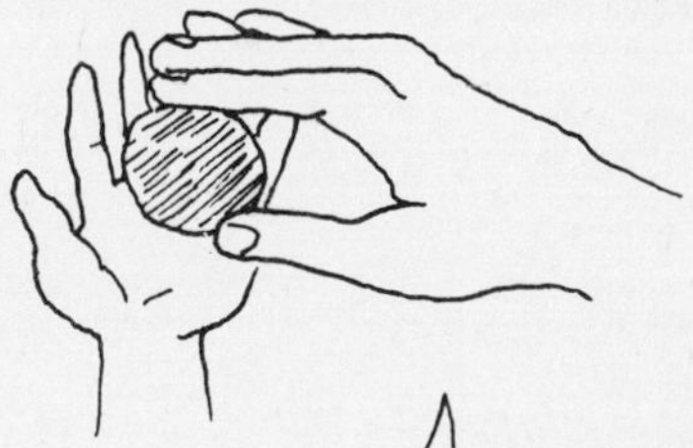

Flatten with a fork.

44

Aggression Cookies

3 cups oatmeal
1½ cups brown sugar
1½ cups flour
1½ cups butter
1½ teaspoons baking powder

Dump all ingredients in large bowl.
Mash it!

Knead it!

Pound it!

The longer and harder you mix it, the better it tastes!
Roll dough into small balls.
Bake on cookie sheet at 350° for 10-12 minutes.

Gingerbread People

2½ cups flour
¾ teaspoon salt
½ teaspoon baking soda
¾ teaspoon ginger
¼ teaspoon nutmeg
⅛ teaspoon allspice
½ cup soft shortening
½ cup brown sugar
½ cup dark molasses
¼ cup water

Sift all dry ingredients together and set aside.

Cream shortening and sugar together in a bowl.

46

Gingerbread People cont'd.

Blend in molasses and water.

Stir in dry ingredients.

Chill dough for 2 hours or overnight in the refrigerator.

Roll dough to ¼ inch thick on a lightly floured board.

Cut dough with gingerbread boy or girl cookie cutter dipped in flour.

Gingerbread People cont'd.

Carefully place gingerbread people, using spatula, on lightly greased cookie sheet.

Before baking decorate eyes, nose, and mouth with raisins, red cinnamon candies, or bits of gumdrops.

Bake 10 minutes at 375.°

Cool cookies on wire rack.

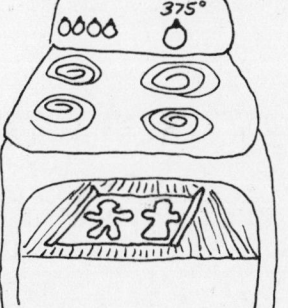

Frost with Creamy Frosting.

Makes 15 gingerbread people.

Peanut Butter Quickies

1 15-ounce can Eagle Brand Milk 
½ cup crunchy peanut butter  
2 cups graham cracker crumbs 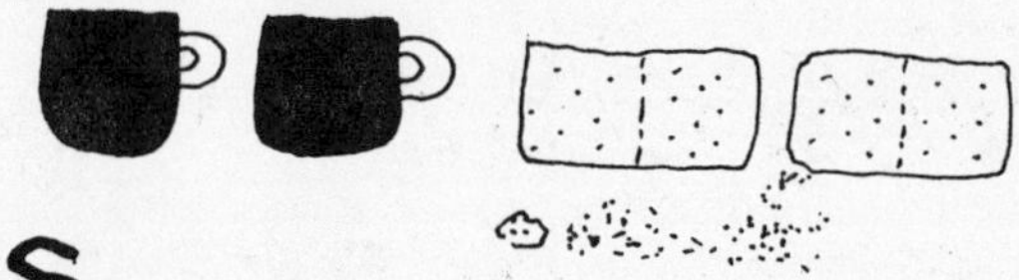
½ cup chopped dates or chocolate chips

Heat oven to 350°

Smash graham crackers to make crumbs. 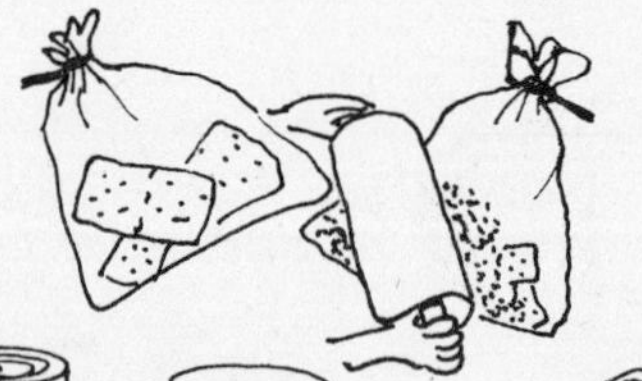
Blend milk and peanut butter until smooth. 
Mix in crumbs and dates.

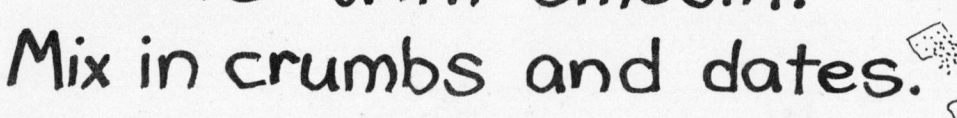

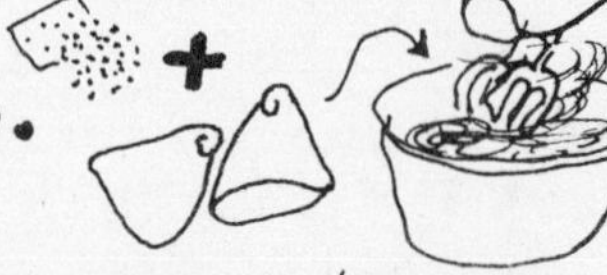

Drop by teaspoon on greased baking sheet. Bake 12-15 minutes. Makes 3 dozen (36).

Macaroons

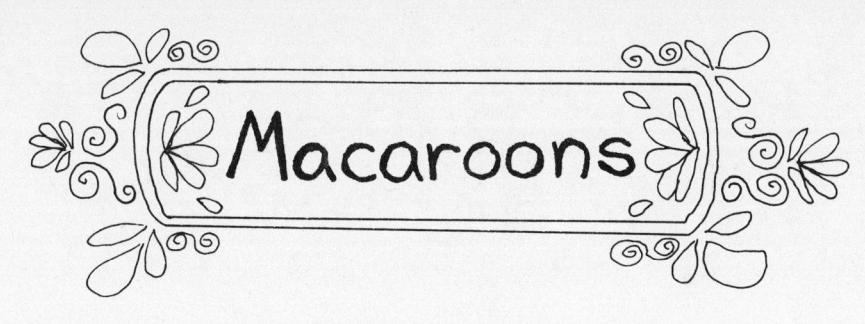

4 egg whites
¾ cup sugar 
1 cup coconut
1½ teaspoons lemon juice 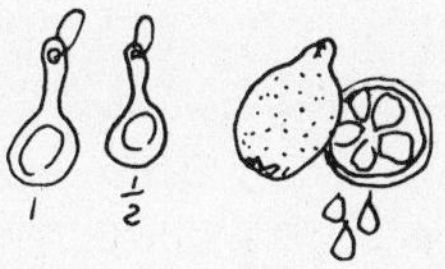
2 teaspoons flour

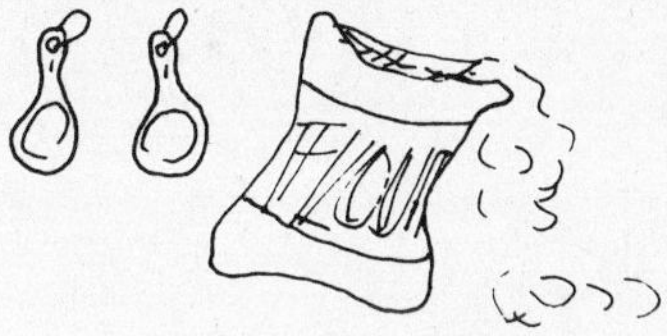

Beat egg whites and sugar.

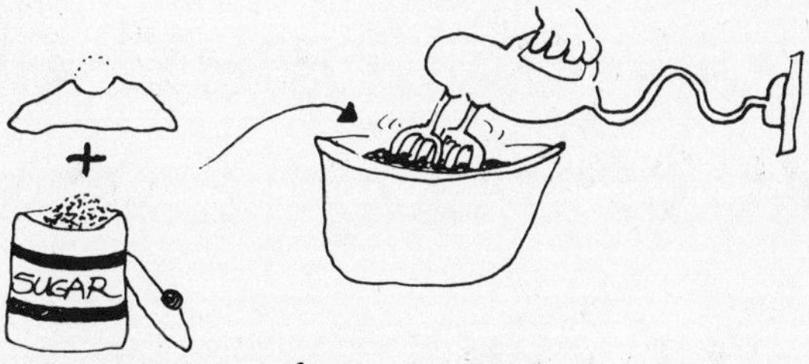

Add remaining ingredients.

Put in cupcake papers.

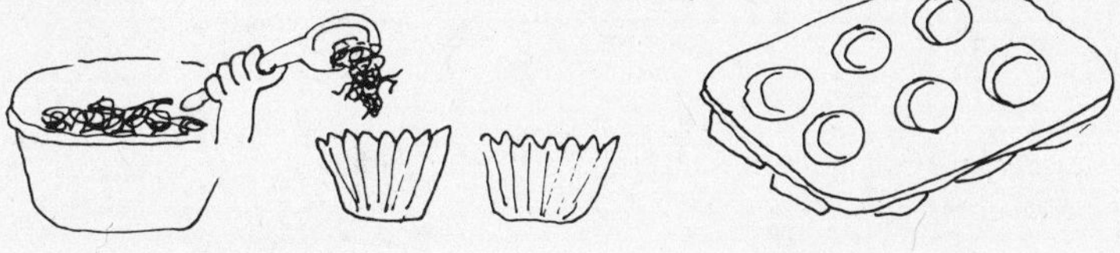

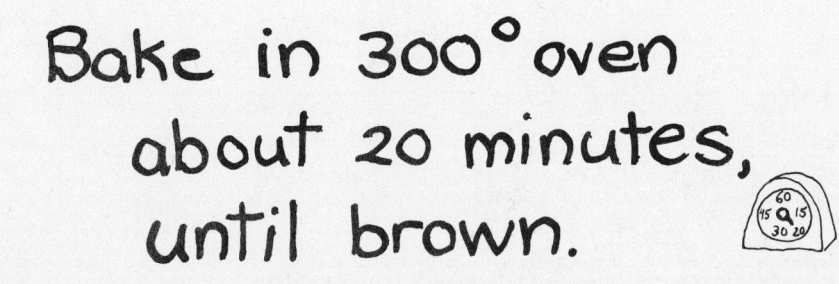

Bake in 300° oven about 20 minutes, until brown.

50

Peanut Butter Cookies

½ cup shortening
½ cup peanut butter
½ cup granulated sugar
½ cup brown sugar
1 egg
1¼ cups flour
½ teaspoon baking powder
¾ teaspoon soda
¼ teaspoon salt

Mix shortening, peanut butter, sugar, and egg thoroughly.

Blend dry ingredients.

Peanut Butter Cookies cont'd.

Stir dry mixture into shortening mixture.

Chill dough.

Roll dough in small balls.

Place 3 inches apart on *lightly greased* baking sheet.

Flatten cookies crisscross style with a fork dipped in flour.

Bake 10 to 12 minutes at 350°.

Makes 3 dozen (36) 2½ inch cookies.

Sunflower Seed Cookies

1 cup margarine

1 cup firmly packed brown sugar

2 eggs

1 teaspoon vanilla

1½ cups flour

¾ teaspoon salt

1 teaspoon soda

3 cups rolled oats

1 cup sunflower seeds

Cream margarine and sugar thoroughly.

Add eggs and vanilla; beat well.

Sunflower Seed Cookies cont'd.

Add flour, salt, soda, and rolled oats.

Mix thoroughly.

Blend in sunflower seeds.

Form into long rolls.

Wrap in clear plastic film and chill thoroughly.

Slice off cookies and bake on ungreased cookie sheet at 350° for 10 minutes.

Makes 9 dozen (108) cookies.

Granola

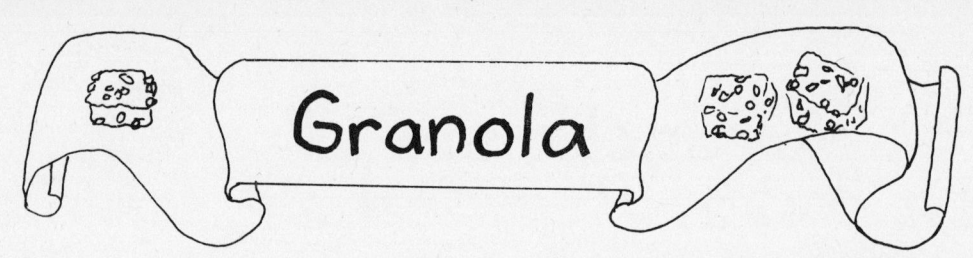

2 ½ cups old-fashioned rolled oats

1 cup shredded coconut

½ cup coarsely chopped almonds

½ cup sesame seeds

½ cup sunflower seeds

½ cup unsweetened wheat germ

Combine these ingredients in a large bowl.

½ cup honey

¼ cup cooking oil

Combine honey and oil.

55

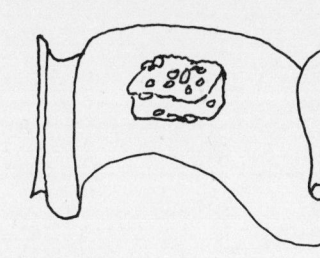

Granola cont'd.

Stir into oat mixture.

Spread out in 13 x 9 x 2 inch baking pan.

Bake in 300° oven until light golden brown – 45 minutes.

Stir with spatula every 15 minutes.

Cool and store in tightly covered container.

Serve as a snack,... or a topping for fruit.

Grandma's Molasses Cookies

1 cup sugar
¾ cup shortening
1 egg
¼ cup molasses
2 cups flour

1 Tablespoon ginger
1 teaspoon cinnamon
2 teaspoons soda
½ teaspoon salt

Cream shortening and sugar.
Add egg and molasses.
Mix well.

Grandma's Molasses Cookies cont'd.

Sift together dry ingredients.

Add to molasses mixture.

Form into small balls.

Roll balls in white sugar and place on cookie sheet.

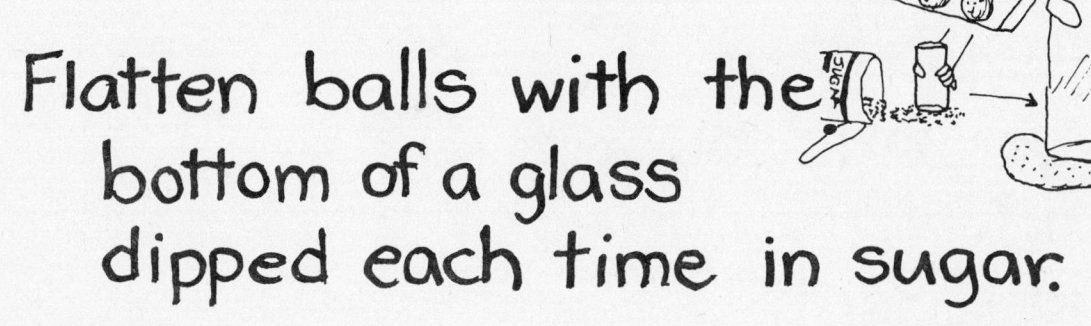

Flatten balls with the bottom of a glass dipped each time in sugar.

Bake for 10 minutes at 375.°

Party Sugar Cookies

1½ cups sifted confectioner's sugar
1 cup butter
1 egg
1 teaspoon vanilla
½ teaspoon almond flavoring
2½ cups flour
1 teaspoon soda
1 teaspoon cream of tartar

Mix sugar and butter.

Add egg, vanilla, and almond; mix well.

Mix dry ingredients in a different bowl.

59

Party Sugar Cookies cont'd.

Add dry ingredients to liquid mixture.

Blend until smooth.

Refrigerate 2 to 3 hours.

Roll dough 3/16" on lightly floured pastry cloth.

Cut with cookie cutter; sprinkle with sugar.

Place on lightly greased baking sheet.

Bake at 375° for 7 to 8 minutes.

Makes 5 dozen (60) 2 inch cookies.

Egg Yolk Paint

Make Party Sugar Cookies.
Roll out a dozen
 at a time (12).
Cut with favorite cookie cutter.
Place cookies on greased
 baking sheet.
Paint with the following:

1 well blended egg yolk
¼ teaspoon water
food coloring

Blend egg yolk and water.
Divide mixture into
 several small cups.
Add a different food coloring
 to each cup.

Egg Yolk Paint cont'd

Make bright colors!
Paint on cookies with
small paint brushes.

Bake cookies, being careful
<u>not</u> to let them brown.

PIERR

62

Creamy Frosting

1/3 cup soft butter

4 cups powdered sugar

2 Tablespoons milk

1 1/2 teaspoons vanilla

food coloring

Cream butter.

Sift in powdered sugar.

Add milk and vanilla.

Mix until creamy.

Divide frosting into several custard cups and tint with food coloring.

Use to decorate cookies.

White Bread

- 2 packages dry yeast
- ½ cup warm water
- 1 ¾ cups warm water
- ½ cup powdered non-fat dry milk
- 2 Tablespoons sugar
- 1 Tablespoon salt
- 3 Tablespoons cooking oil
- 5 ½ to 6 ½ cups flour

Sprinkle yeast into ½ cup warm water, in large warm bowl.

Stir until yeast is dissolved.

White Bread cont'd.

Add remaining water, powdered milk, sugar, salt, oil, and 2 cups of flour.

Beat until smooth.

Add remaining flour gradually, stirring with wooden spoon until you have a soft dough.

* Round up into a ball and divide dough into 2 equal parts.
(or several if you are making small individual loaves of bread.)

White Bread cont'd.

Knead 10 minutes until dough is smooth.

Cover with plastic wrap, then a towel.

Let rest for 20 minutes.

Punch down. Shape dough into loaves.

Place in two greased 8½ x 4½ inch bread pans, or 12 inch loaf pans.

Brush surface of dough with oil.

White Bread cont'd.

Cover pans loosely with oiled waxed paper, then plastic wrap.

Put in cold refrigerator for 24 hours.

Remove pans from refrigerator. Uncover.

Let stand for 10 minutes. Bake at 400° for 30 to 40 minutes for large pans, or 375° for 25 minutes for small pans.

Remove bread from pans. Brush top with margarine. Cool on racks.

* Special Cool Rise Method

Honey Whole Wheat Bread

2 packages active dry yeast
3 cups whole wheat flour
½ cup powdered non-fat dry milk
1 Tablespoon salt

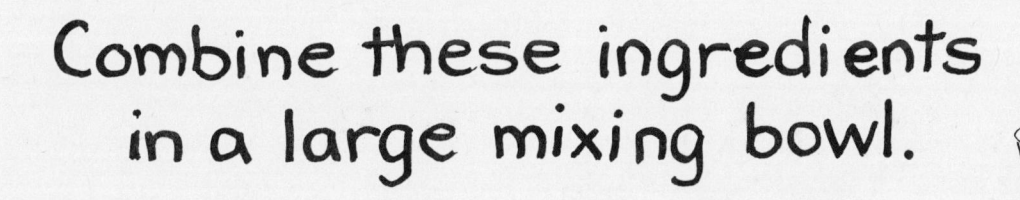

Combine these ingredients in a large mixing bowl.

3 cups water
½ cup honey
2 Tablespoons cooking oil

Heat in saucepan until warm.

Honey Whole Wheat Bread cont'd.

1 cup whole wheat flour
4 to 4½ cups white flour

Put warm liquid over flour mixture.

Blend until smooth.

Stir in additional 1 cup whole wheat flour. And gradually stir in remaining white flour until you have a soft dough.

Follow Special Cool Rise Method for raising bread. * (page 65)

Bake 2 loaves at 375°, 40 to 50 min.

Corn Bread

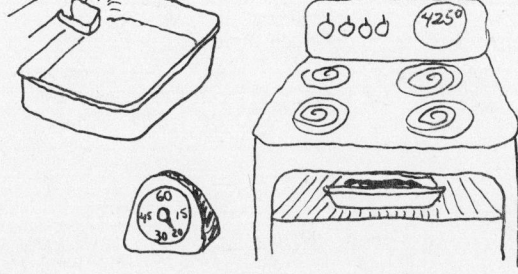

¾ cup corn meal
1 cup flour
¼ cup molasses
3 teaspoons baking powder
¾ teaspoon salt

Mix and sift above ingredients together. Then add:

¾ cup milk
1 egg, well beaten
2 Tablespoons melted shortening

Bake in buttered pan, 8 by 8 inches at 425° for 20 minutes.

Serve warm with honey — or molasses.

Pumpkin Bread

1 cup shortening
2 ¾ cups sugar

3 eggs
2 cups pumpkin

3 ½ cups flour
½ teaspoon baking powder
1 teaspoon soda

1 teaspoon cloves
1 teaspoon nutmeg
1 teaspoon allspice
1 teaspoon cinnamon
1 teaspoon salt

¾ cup chopped nuts

Pumpkin Bread cont'd.

Cream shortening and sugar together in mixing bowl.

Add eggs and beat until fluffy.

Add pumpkin.

Gradually beat in flour, salt, baking powder, soda, and spices.

Mix well and add nuts.

Put in two bread pans.

Bake at 325° for one hour.

Aunt Nora's Buckskin Bread

1 quart sifter of flour
2 heaping teaspoons baking powder
salt in hand (about 1 teaspoon)
2 heaping Tablespoons shortening
1½ cups water

Sift flour and baking powder into large bowl.

Add salt and shortening.

Mix it up well with your hands.

Add water until dough is soft.

Aunt Nora's Buckskin Bread cont'd.

Knead dough on floured cookie sheet.

Shape dough into one large oblong, flat loaf.

Bake at 450° for 20 minutes.

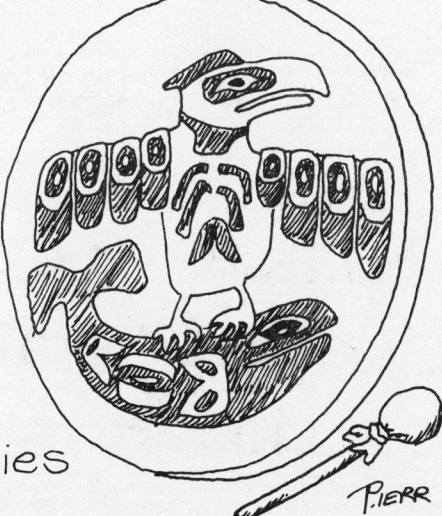

Serve hot with butter and jam.

— Nora Barker —
Head Drummer and Singer for Makah Ceremonies

Indian Fry Bread

2 cups flour
4 teaspoons baking powder

1 teaspoon salt
2/3 cup warm water

Combine flour, baking powder, and salt.

Add water to make dough the consistency of bread.

Tear off balls of dough.

Roll out on a board lightly dusted with flour until each ball is flat and thin.

Indian Fry Bread cont'd.

Punch a hole in the center of each piece.

Fry one at a time in hot fat 2 or 3 inches deep.

Drain on a piece of absorbent paper.

Pour honey on the top.

Eat while hot... and smile!

Many Muffins Mix

2 cups dates, cut up
5 teaspoons baking soda
2 cups boiling water
1 cup butter
2 cups brown sugar
4 eggs, beaten
1 quart buttermilk
1 teaspoon salt
1 cup chopped walnuts
5 cups flour
4 cups oatmeal

Mix soda and dates in small mixing bowl.

Many Muffins Mix cont'd.

Cover dates with boiling water and let them cool.

Cream sugar and butter in large mixing bowl.

Add beaten eggs and buttermilk. Blend well and add dates.

Add flour, salt, nuts, and oatmeal.

Stir just until dry ingredients are moistened.

Fill buttered muffin pans $\frac{2}{3}$ full.

Bake at 375° for 20 minutes.

Serve hot with jam or honey.

This batter can be refrigerated for a couple of months.

Gingerbread

2 cups whole wheat flour

1½ teaspoons baking soda

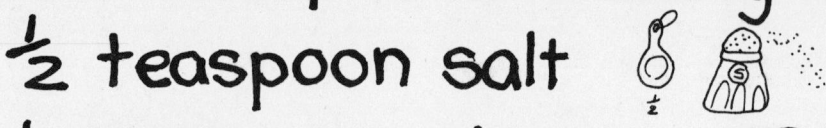

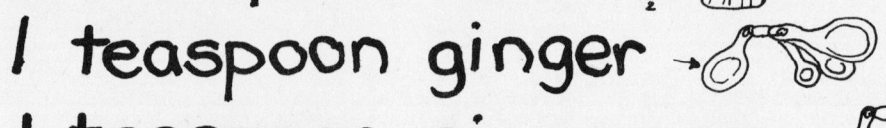

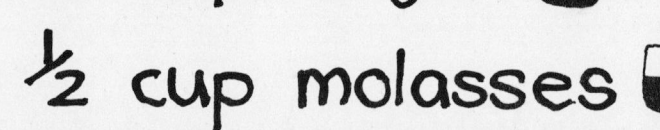

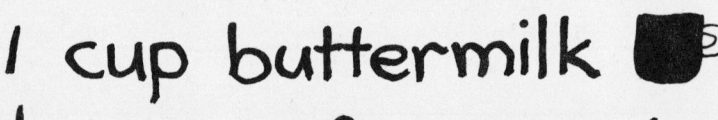

½ teaspoon salt

1 teaspoon ginger

1 teaspoon cinnamon

2 eggs, beaten

½ cup sugar

½ cup molasses

1 cup buttermilk

½ cup soft margarine

applesauce

Sift together flour, soda, salt, spices, and sugar.

Gingerbread cont'd.

Beat eggs until foamy.

Add molasses, buttermilk, and margarine.

Gradually stir into flour-sugar mixture. Stir just until you can't see any more flour.

Butter an 8 inch square baking dish.

Pour batter in dish and bake at 350° for 30 minutes.

Serve warm with applesauce on top. (page 111)

80

Swedish Pancakes

1 cup flour
2 Tablespoons sugar
¼ teaspoon salt
4 eggs
3 cups milk
butter

Sift together flour, sugar, and salt.

Beat eggs.

Add eggs and milk gradually to flour-sugar mixture.

Brush fry pan with butter.

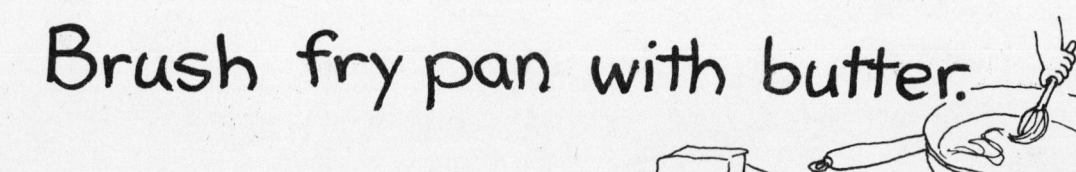

81

Swedish Pancakes cont'd.

Pour small amount of batter into hot frying pan.

Fry on both sides until nicely browned.

Beat batter before making next pancake.

Serve pancakes rolled up with jam.

Sift powdered sugar on top.

Wheat Pancakes

2 cups unmilled wheat grain

3 teaspoons baking powder

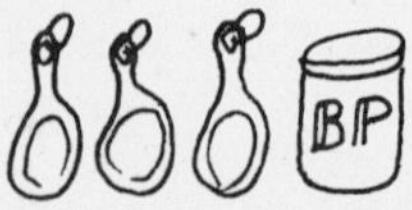

½ teaspoon salt

1 Tablespoon brown sugar

1 well beaten egg

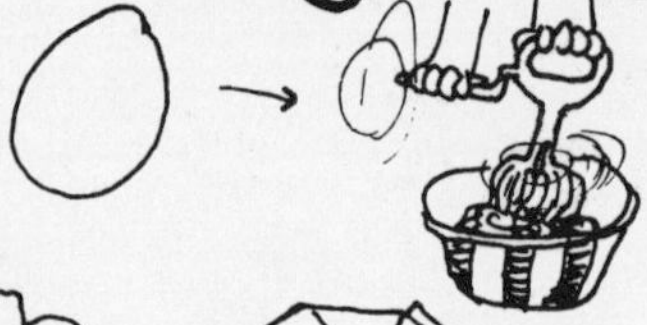

1¼ cups milk

2 Tablespoons salad oil

Spread wheat on tray and remove hulls.

Pulverize in blender.

Sift to remove unwanted particles.

Wheat Pancakes cont'd.

Measure out 2 cups flour.

Sift flour, baking powder, sugar, and salt into a bowl.

Add egg, milk, and oil.

Beat until smooth.

Grease skillet and pour in small amounts of pancake batter.

Flip pancakes over.

Fry until golden brown on both sides.

Potato Pancakes

4 peeled potatoes
1 beaten egg
4 Tablespoons pancake flour
1 small chopped onion
salt
pepper

Grate peeled potatoes.

Mix egg, flour, salt, and pepper with potatoes.

Shape mixture into cakes. Fry until crisp and brown. Drain on paper towel and keep warm until ready to eat.

Serve with warm applesauce.

French Toast

4 eggs
1/2 cup milk
1/2 teaspoon salt
1/2 teaspoon cinnamon
1/2 teaspoon vanilla
8 slices whole wheat bread

Crack eggs into bowl; beat them slightly.

Stir in milk, salt, vanilla, and cinnamon.

Dip bread in mixture on both sides.

Fry in oil until brown on both sides.

Serve with brown sugar and cinnamon.

Waffles

2 cups flour

2 teaspoons baking powder

½ teaspoon salt

3 eggs

1¼ cups milk

⅓ cup salad oil

2 teaspoons sugar

Turn waffle iron to "ON."

Crack eggs into a mixing bowl.

Beat eggs until foamy.

Add milk and oil and continue beating for about one minute.

Waffles cont'd.

Sift dry ingredients into the bowl and mix until well blended.

Pour ½ cup batter into hot waffle iron.

Bake.

Serve immediately with fruit, honey, or syrup.

88

Soft Pretzels

1 package yeast
1 ½ cups warm water
1 teaspoon salt
1 Tablespoon sugar
4 cups flour
1 egg, beaten
coarse salt

Measure warm water into large mixing bowl.

Sprinkle on yeast and stir until it looks soft.

Add salt, sugar, and flour.

Soft Pretzels cont'd.

Mix and knead dough.

Every child gets
  small ball of dough
  to roll and twist into
  letters, numerals,
  snakes, and things.

Grease cookie sheets.

Lay twisted pretzels
  on cookie sheets.

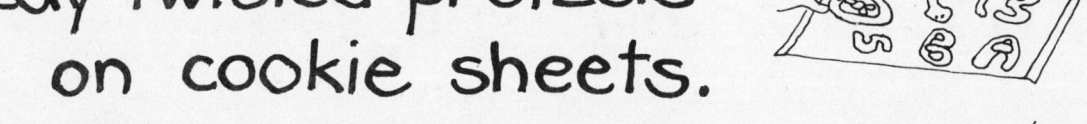

Brush pretzels with
  beaten egg and sprinkle
  with coarse salt.

Bake at 425° for 12
  to 15 minutes.

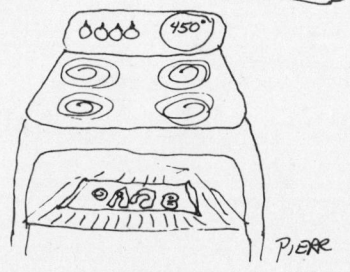

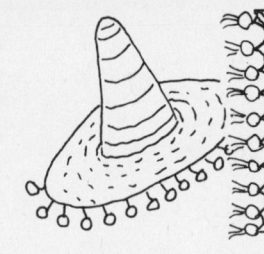

Sopapillas

4 cups flour
1 teaspoon salt
4 teaspoons baking powder
2 teaspoons lard
1-2 cups water

Mix dry ingredients in a bowl.
Then add lard.

Add water and mix well.

Roll out small amounts of dough and cut in four pieces.

Fry in very hot fat.

Sopapillas cont'd.

Turn sopapillas over quickly and watch them poof up!

Remove to paper towel as soon as they are golden brown.

Eat with honey.

92

Tortillas

3 cups flour
1 teaspoon baking powder
½ teaspoon salt
2 Tablespoons lard
1-2 cups water

Mix dry ingredients.

Add lard and mix well.

Add water a little at a time.

Knead dough until smooth.

Roll out small amounts of dough with rolling pin.

Cook in hot fry pan for about one minute on each side.

Individual Graham Cracker Crusts

24 graham crackers

4 Tablespoons sugar
¾ cup melted butter
12 foil muffin cups

Crush graham crackers in plastic bag.

Add sugar and butter and mix thoroughly.

Press crumb mixture into muffin cups.

Fill with fruit pudding or Creamy Pumpkin Pie Filling. (pages 123 and 99)

94

Individual Pizzas

8 English muffins, cut in half

1 cup tomato sauce

1 teaspoon oregano

1 teaspoon sweet basil

2 teaspoons minced onion

1 cup shredded mozzarella cheese

1 can black olives, sliced

1 can mushroom pieces

2 smoked link sausages

Combine tomato sauce, onion, oregano, and basil in dish.

Individual Pizzas cont'd.

Each child spreads own muffin half with tomato sauce mixture,

then chooses any variety of ingredients to sprinkle on top.

or   or

Bake pizzas at 450° for about 10 minutes.

Sprinkle with grated cheese and return to oven until the cheese melts.

96

Pumpkin Pie

2 eggs, slightly beaten
1½ cups pumpkin
¾ cup firmly-packed brown sugar
½ teaspoon salt
1 teaspoon cinnamon
½ teaspoon ginger
½ teaspoon cloves
1 can evaporated milk

Combine all ingredients.

Pour into a 9 inch pie shell.

Bake at 425° for 15 minutes, then at 350° for 45 minutes.

Patting Pie Crust

1½ cups flour
½ teaspoon salt
1 Tablespoon sugar
½ cup cooking oil
2 Tablespoons milk

Sift flour, salt, and sugar together into 9-inch pie pan.

Add milk and oil.

Mix with a fork or your fingers.

Pat the dough out to cover the pie pan.

Creamy Pumpkin Pie Filling

1 can pumpkin
 (3 cups cooked pumpkin)
1 jar marshmallow creme
1 teaspoon cinnamon 
½ teaspoon ginger 
¼ teaspoon salt

Cook pumpkin, marshmallow creme, spices, and salt until mixture is creamy.

Let cool.

Beat chilled carton of "Cool Whip" until fluffy.

Fold into pumpkin mixture.

Creamy Pumpkin Pie Filling cont'd.

Spoon mixture into individual pie shells.
(page 94)

Top with whipped cream.

100

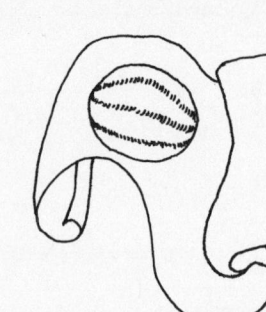

Melon Ball Salad

1 watermelon

1 cantelope

1 honeydew melon

2 bananas

1 cup seedless grapes

3 Tablespoons frozen orange juice concentrate

2 Tablespoons frozen lemonade concentrate

Scoop out 3 cups watermelon balls and all the cantelope and honeydew balls you can get.

Melon Ball Salad cont'd.

Combine melon balls and grapes in large mixing bowl.

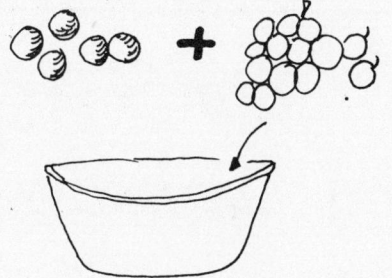

Add the frozen juices and mix well.

Slice and add bananas just before serving.

Marshmallow Fruit Salad

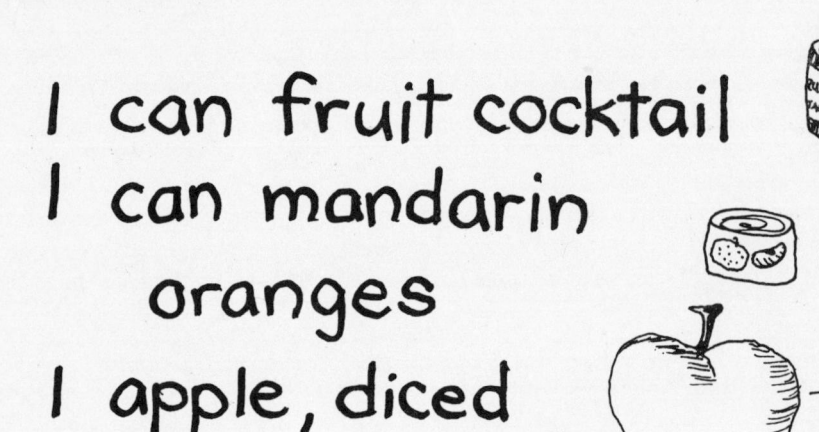

1 can fruit cocktail

1 can mandarin oranges

1 apple, diced

1 pear, diced

1 cup miniature marshmallows

1 banana, sliced

1 cup other fruit (grapes or peaches)

¼ cup walnuts, broken up

½ cup mayonnaise

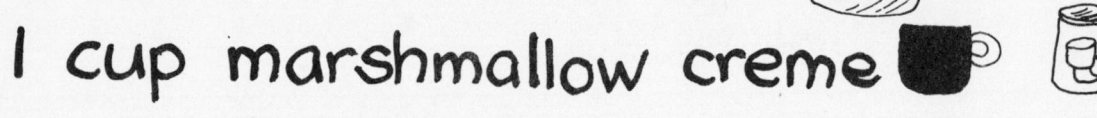

1 cup marshmallow creme

Drain fruit cocktail and oranges.

Marshmallow Fruit Salad cont'd.

Pour fruit into a bowl.

Add diced apples and pears, marshmallows, banana, other fruit, and walnuts.

Mix with a spoon.

Combine mayonnaise and marshmallow creme in small bowl.

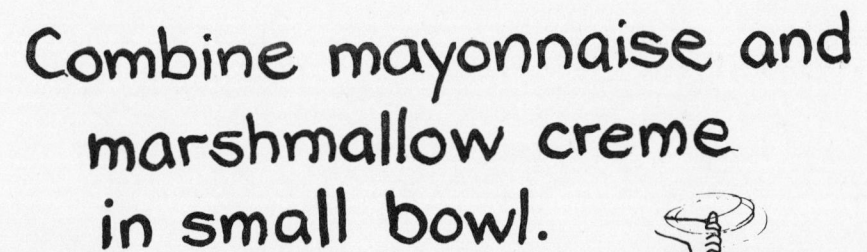

Mix well.

Add to fruit salad.

Stir until blended.

Chill and serve.

Fruit Salad

1 cup mandarin oranges
1 cup pineapple
1 cup miniature marshmallows
1 cup coconut
1 cup sour cream

Combine all ingredients in a large bowl.

Mix well.

Chill in the refrigerator for several hours or overnight.

Carrot - Coconut Salad

1 cup flaked coconut

6 raw carrots

½ cup raisins

2 Tablespoons lemon juice

¼ cup mayonnaise

Scrub carrots with vegetable brush.

Grate carrots into a bowl.

Stir in coconut and and raisins.

Add mayonnaise and mix well.

Chill before serving.

Tossed Vegetable Salad

lettuce
2 carrots
red cabbage
1 cucumber
2 tomatoes
2 small white onions
alfalfa sprouts

Wash and drain all vegetables.

Tear lettuce.

Scrub carrots.

Cut carrots, cucumber, tomatoes, and part of red cabbage. Into small pieces.

Tossed Vegetable Salad cont'd.

Remove skin and cut onions.

Combine all vegetables in a large salad bowl.

Toss the vegetables to mix.

Serve with different kinds of salad dressings and whole wheat crackers.

Apple Salad

1 cup diced apples

1 cup diced celery

½ cup broken walnuts

½ cup raisins

½ cup mayonnaise

2 Tablespoons milk

Mix apples, celery, walnuts, and raisins together.

Combine mayonnaise and milk.

Add to apple mixture.

Stir it up.

Blender Applesauce

3 tart apples
¼ cup honey

Peel apples.

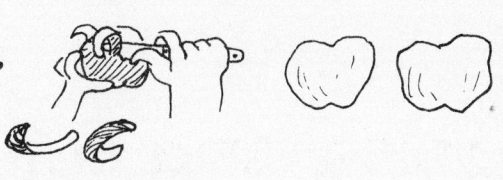

Cut each apple into 4 pieces.
Remove seeds.

Put the apples into blender with honey and a small amount of water.

Blend until smooth.

Eat applesauce immediately.

Applesauce

6 sour apples
½ cup honey
1 cup water

Wash apples and cut into quarters.

Put pieces into large saucepan or electric skillet.

Add water.

Cover pan and cook apples slowly over medium heat, about 30 minutes until they are squishy.

Stir occasionally.

Applesauce cont'd.

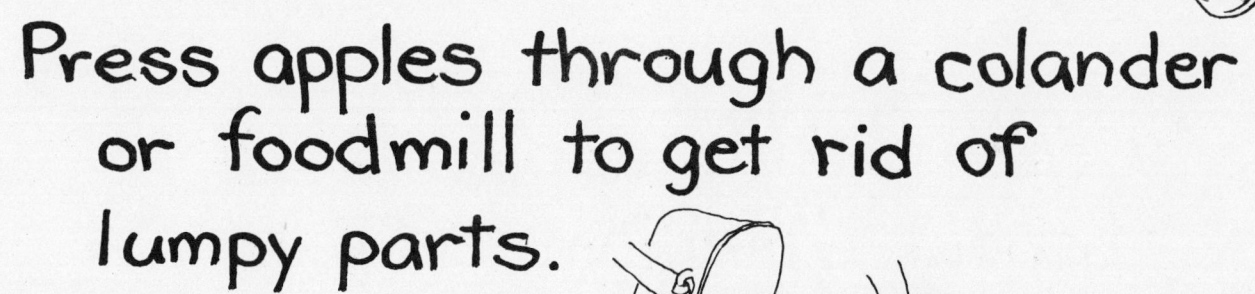

Press apples through a colander or foodmill to get rid of lumpy parts.

Add honey and a few drops of red food coloring if you want rosy red applesauce.

Sprinkle with cinnamon and nutmeg.

Serve warm on Gingerbread (page 79) or Potato Pancakes. (page 85)

Apple Crisp

4 cups baking apples
(about 6 medium
   apples)
¾ cup packed
   brown sugar
½ cup flour
½ cup rolled oats
¾ teaspoon cinnamon
¾ teaspoon nutmeg
⅓ cup butter

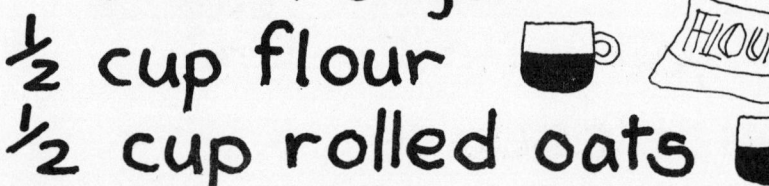

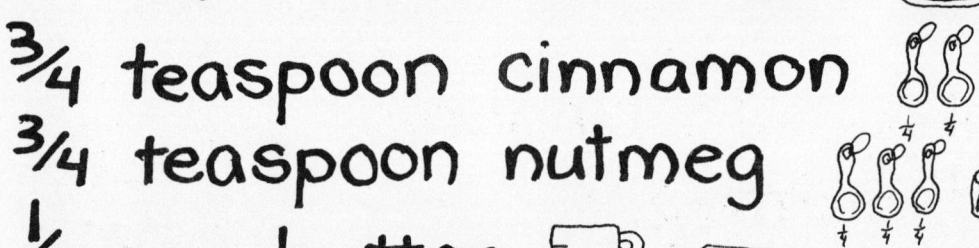

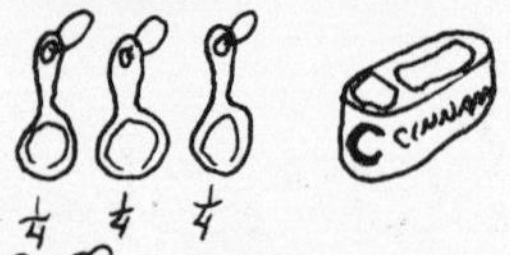

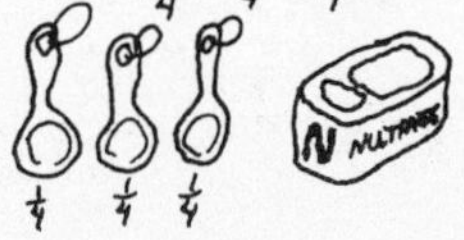

Peel and slice apples.

Put sliced apples
   in a greased 8
   inch square pan.

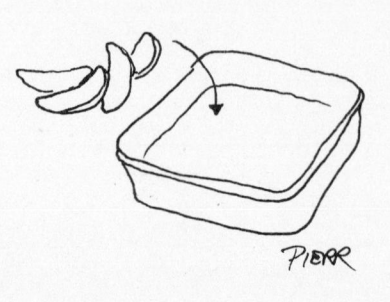

Apple Crisp cont'd.

Blend flour, oats, cinnamon, nutmeg, and butter together until mixture is crumbly.

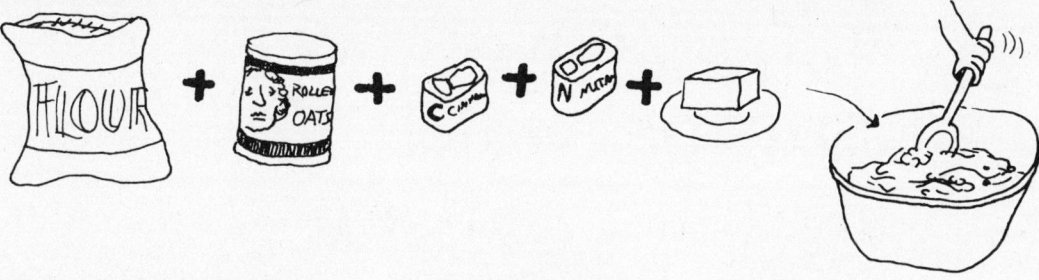

Spread over apples.

Bake 35 minutes at 350° until topping is golden brown.

Caramel Apples

6 small apples

6 popsicle sticks

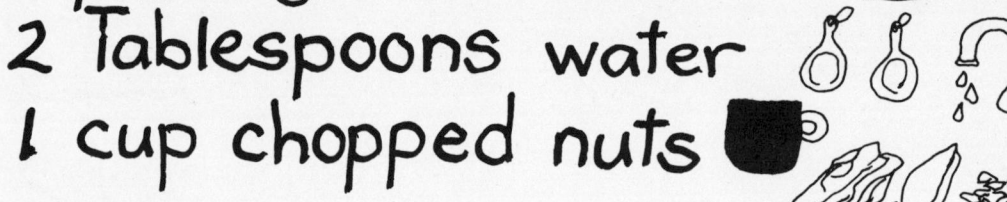

1 package of caramels

2 Tablespoons water

1 cup chopped nuts

Wash the apples.

Dry them.

Remove their stems.

Stick wooden popsicle sticks into stem ends of apples.

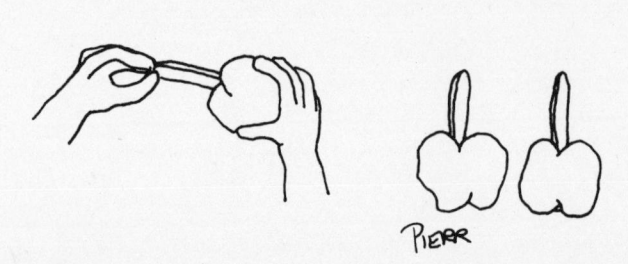

Caramel Apples cont'd.

Chop up nuts and put them in a bowl.

Melt caramels in a heavy saucepan, adding 2 tablespoons of water.

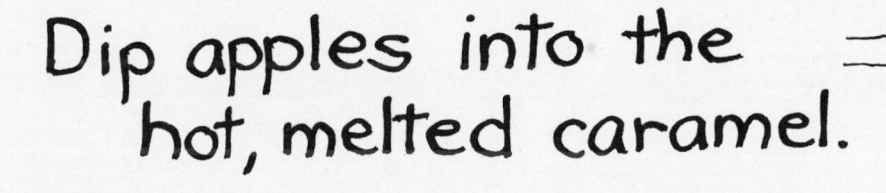

Dip apples into the hot, melted caramel.

Roll apples in chopped nuts.

Let cool on greased waxed paper.

Fruit Jell

½ cup cold water
1 envelope unflavored gelatin
1 6 ounce can frozen fruit juice
1 cup cold water
¼ cup honey
1 can mandarin oranges or other fruit

Put ½ cup water in pan.

Sprinkle gelatin in and cook over low heat until gelatin is dissolved.

Stir constantly.

Remove from stove and stir in fruit juice, 1 cup water, and honey.

Add canned or fresh fruit.

Refrigerate until set.

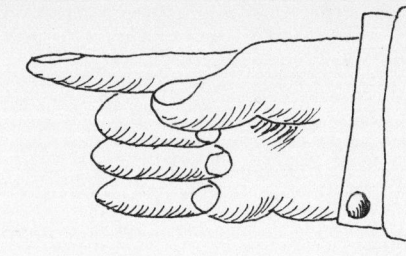

Finger Jello

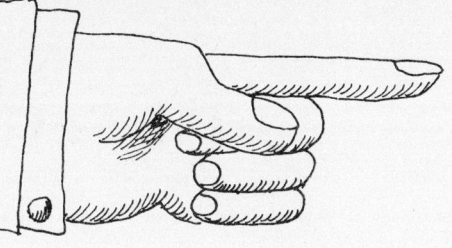

3 packages flavored jello

3 cups boiling water

4 packages knox gelatine

1 cup water

Dissolve jello in boiling water.

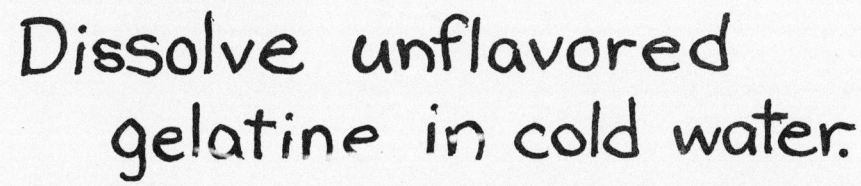

Dissolve unflavored gelatine in cold water.

Mix everything together.

Add 2 tablespoons lemon juice and stir.

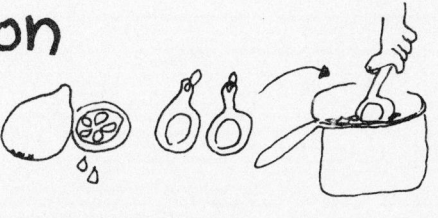

Pour mixture into large cake pan.

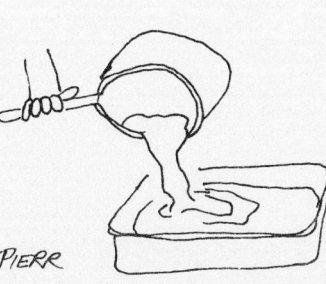

Finger Jello cont'd.

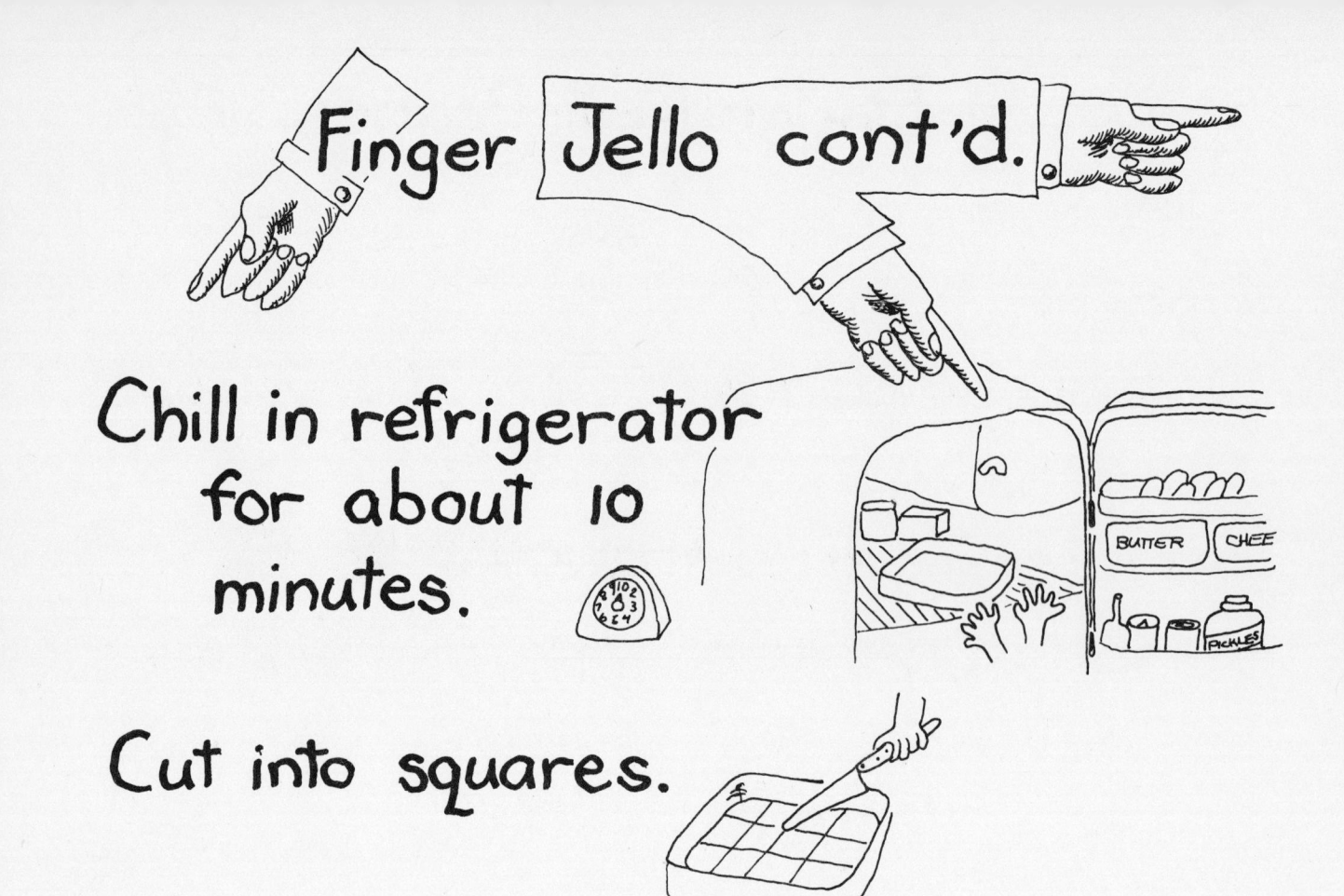

Chill in refrigerator for about 10 minutes.

Cut into squares.

Eat with your fingers!

Walnut-Stuffed Prunes

1 pound bag of dried prunes

1 cup broken walnuts

18 large marshmallows cut in pieces

¼ cup sugar

Cut sides of prunes and remove pits.

Stuff with walnut and marshmallow pieces.

Roll in sugar.

Store in covered container in a cool place for several days.

Eat for snacks.

Things to do with Bananas

- **BANANA SANDWICHES**

    Slice bananas.

    Spread one piece with peanut butter and top with other banana piece.

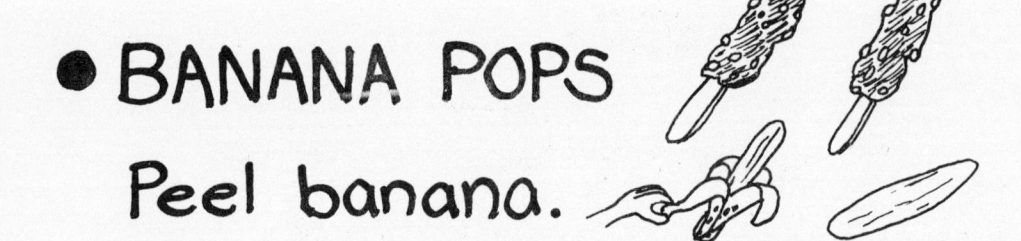

- **BANANA POPS**

    Peel banana.

    Insert a popsicle stick.

    Dip banana in chocolate syrup.

    Roll in walnut bits.

    Freeze for 1 or 2 hours.

More Things to do with Bananas

- ## FRIED BANANAS

    Cut bananas in half.

    Heat enough oil to cover bottom of frying pan.

    Brown bananas on one side.

    Turn, and brown on other side.

    Serve with brown sugar and lemon juice or pancake syrup.

- ## BANANA MILKSHAKE

    Blend sliced bananas and milk or ice cream in a blender.

Coconut Pudding

½ cup cornstarch
3 Tablespoons sugar
⅛ teaspoon salt
2 cups coconut milk

Combine cornstarch, sugar, and salt.

Add ½ cup of coconut milk and blend until smooth.

Heat remaining coconut milk in heavy saucepan over low heat; add cornstarch mixture gradually, stirring constantly, until thickened.

Coconut Pudding cont'd.

Pour into a 9 by 9 inch pan.

Cool until firm in refrigerator.

Cut into squares and eat with your fingers.

African Slush Punch

4 cups sugar
6 cups water

1 12-ounce can frozen orange juice 
1 6-ounce can frozen lemonade 
1 6-ounce can water 
1 large can unsweetened pineapple juice 
5 mashed bananas 
3 quarts Canada Dry Gingerale

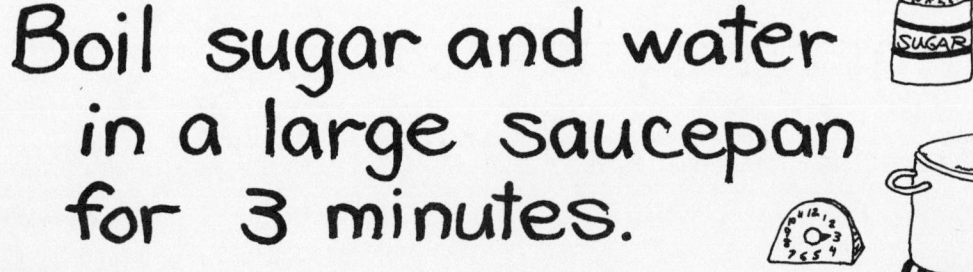

Boil sugar and water in a large saucepan for 3 minutes.

African Slush Punch cont'd.

Cool.

Mash bananas in blender, and combine in large container with fruit juices and the 6 ounce can water.

Add sugar mixture and blend well.

Freeze for at least 24 hours.

Remove from freezer one hour before serving. Mash to a pulp.

Add gingerale, mix, and serve at Parent night.

Fruit Shake

1 cup powdered non-fat dry milk

3 cups chilled fruit juice

1 Tablespoon sugar

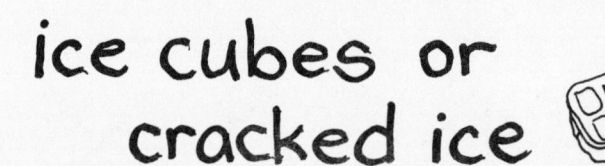

ice cubes or cracked ice

Combine ingredients in a blender.

Blend until creamy.

Serves 6.

Essie's Supershake

2 sliced bananas
1 cup milk
¼ cup wheat germ
¼ cup broken walnuts
¼ cup chopped dates
2 ice cubes

Combine all ingredients, except milk, in a blender.

Turn on HIGH until ingredients are blended.

Add milk and blend once more.

Pour into glasses and serve immediately.

Witches' Caldron

4 cups cranberry cocktail

4 cups apple cider

2 cinnamon sticks

½ teaspoon ground nutmeg

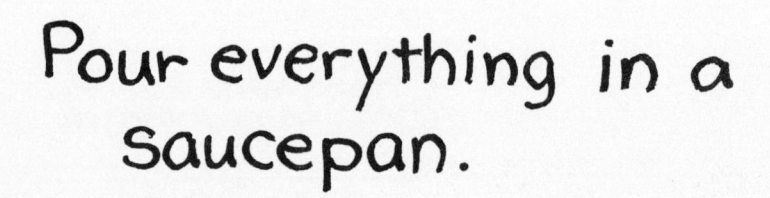

Pour everything in a saucepan.

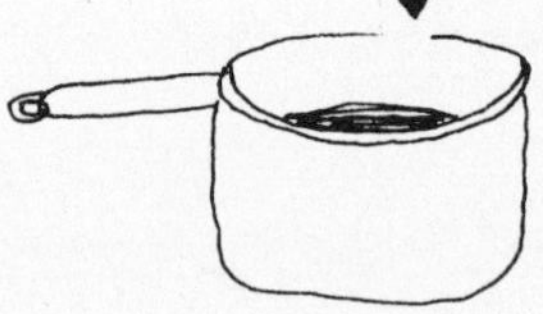

Heat and simmer with cover on pan for 10 minutes.

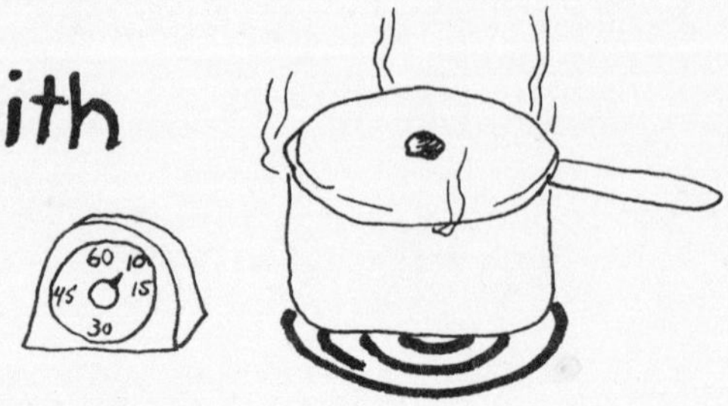

Serve hot.

Hot Cider and Cinnamon Sticks

5 cups brown sugar

¼ teaspoon salt

2 quarts cider

1 teaspoon whole allspice

1 teaspoon whole cloves

1 3-inch cinnamon stick

dash of nutmeg

Combine sugar, salt, and cider in a large saucepan.

Tie spices up in a piece of cheesecloth.

Add to cider.

Slowly bring to boil; simmer with pan covered for 20 minutes.

Serve immediately. Makes 10 to 12 servings.

Egg Nog

15 eggs

2 quarts milk

1 cup sugar

3 Tablespoons vanilla

nutmeg

Crack eggs.
Separate egg whites and beat until stiff.
Color with food coloring.

Beat egg yolks until foamy.
Add milk, sugar, and vanilla. Mix well.
Pour into glasses.
Top with egg whites and sprinkle on nutmeg.

You may save half the egg whites to make Macaroons. (page 50)

Grape Jelly

2 cups grape juice

3½ cups sugar

½ bottle fruit pectin

Mix sugar and juice together in a saucepan over high heat.

Bring mixture to boil, stirring constantly.

Stir in pectin at once, then bring to a full boil and boil hard for one minute, stirring constantly.

Remove from heat, skim off the foam and pour jelly into paper cups.

Take home as presents.

Cranberry Relish

4 cups cranberries

2 oranges

1½ cups sugar

Wash cranberries and oranges.

Cut oranges into quarters.
Take out core.

Put cranberries and oranges through a food grinder.

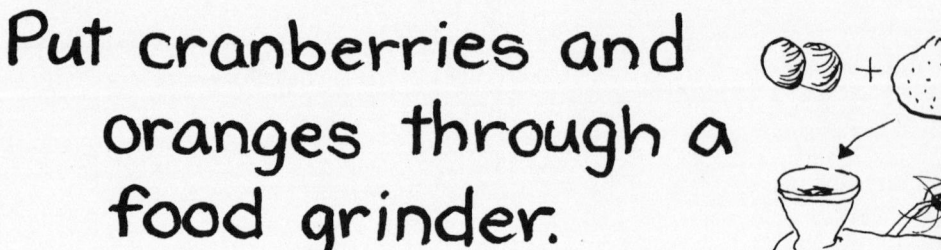

Add sugar and mix well.

Cranberry Relish cont'd.

Put cranberry relish in baby food jars.

Take home to family at Thanksgiving time.

Cooking a Pumpkin

Cut pumpkin in half and pull out the seeds and scrape out the strings.

Cut pumpkin up in several pieces.

Put these pieces in a colander set inside a large pan.

Put water in just to bottom of colander.

Cover pan and heat to a boil.

Continue cooking over medium high heat for 30 to 40 minutes until pumpkin soft.

Peel off skin.

Put pumpkin through a food mill.

Use to make Pumpkin Pie or bread. (Pages 97 and 71.)

Toasted Pumpkin Seeds

Scoop out the seeds from a pumpkin.

Wash the seeds.

Pat dry on a paper towel.

Grease cookie sheet with 1 to 2 Tablespoons melted butter.

Spread seeds on cookie sheet.

Sprinkle with salt.

Bake in 300° oven for 1 hour, until seeds are golden brown and crispy.

Sprouts

2 Tablespoons alfalfa seeds or mung beans

one-quart jar
cheesecloth
rubberband

Place seeds in jar.

Fill jar about half full with water and let it soak overnight.

The next day cover jar with cheesecloth held in place by a rubberband.

Pour off the water.

Sprouts cont'd.

Rinse beans or seeds well with fresh water.

Rinse twice a day and drain well. Place jar on its side with a paper towel over it to cut out the light.

On the third or fourth day expose sprouts to the light to turn green.

The sprouts will now be about one inch long and ready to eat.

Keep sprouts fresh in refrigerator.

What to do with Sprouts?

Eat them raw as a nutritious snack.

Put them in salads.

Combine with egg dishes

soups

casseroles

Put them on melted cheese sandwiches.

Chicken Soup with Rice

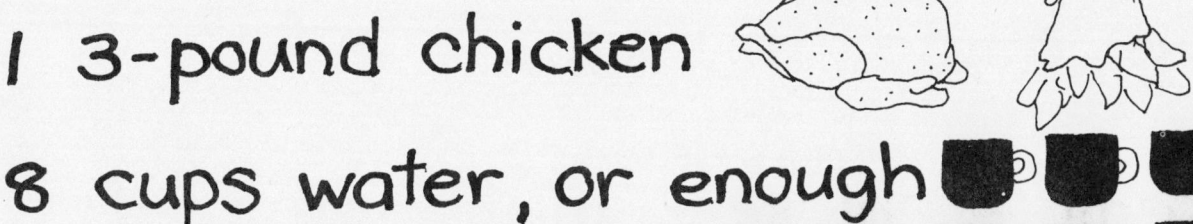

1 3-pound chicken 
8 cups water, or enough to cover chicken 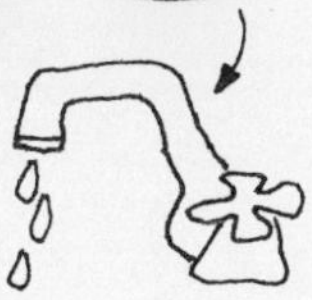 
1 Tablespoon salt
1 carrot  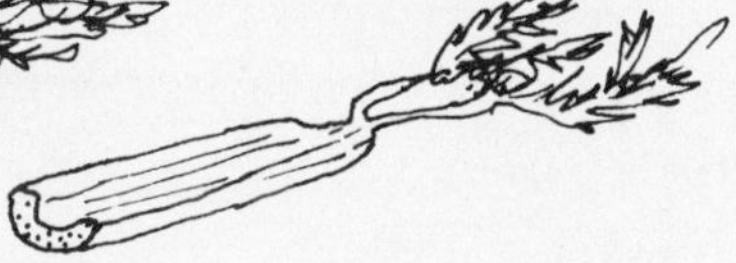
1 celery stalk
½ bay leaf

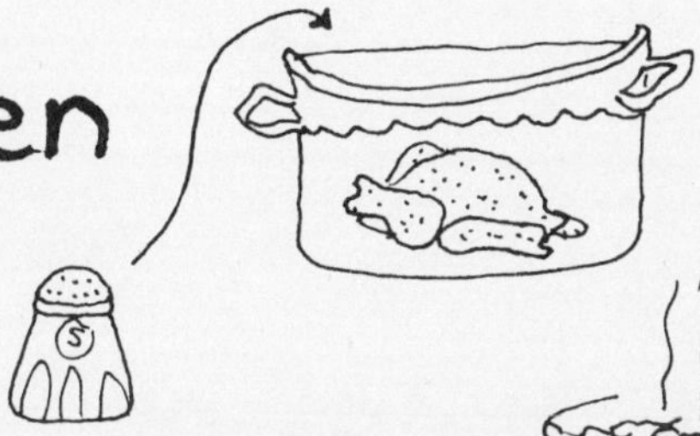

Place whole chicken in a saucepan with water. Add salt and bring to boil.

Add carrot, celery and bay leaf. Simmer for about 40 minutes.

Chicken Soup with Rice cont'd.

Set aside and cool.

Remove chicken meat from bones.

Strain broth.

Save chicken and broth and bones to examine later.

Heat broth in large pan.

Add enough chicken bouillon cubes to make it taste good.

141

Chicken Soup with Rice cont'd.

Add some of the chicken meat, 1 cup chopped celery, and ½ cup rice.

Cook until celery and rice are tender. (About 30 minutes.)

Serve with whole wheat crackers.

Stone Soup

1 large, very clean stone

4 cups water

3 large carrots

3 potatoes

2 onions

1 can tomatoes

1 can corn

1 can peas

4 teaspoons beef bouillon

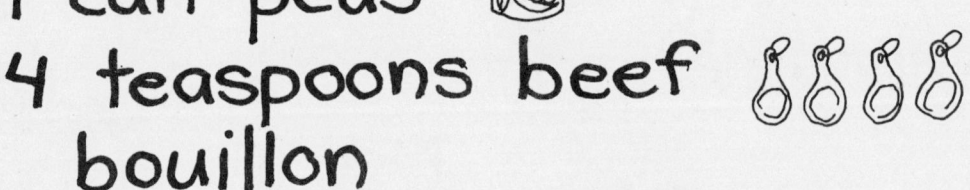

dash of salt

Heat water in a large pot.

Stone Soup cont'd.

Add the stone.

Peel and cut up carrots, potatoes, onions and celery.

Boil these ingredients until soft.

Add tomatoes, corn, peas, and bouillon.

Add salt and boil 10 minutes.

Remove the stone.

Serve with crackers.

"Stone Soup" is a popular folk tale.

Isabelle's Fish Stew

1 salmon fish head cut in half

several pieces of salmon

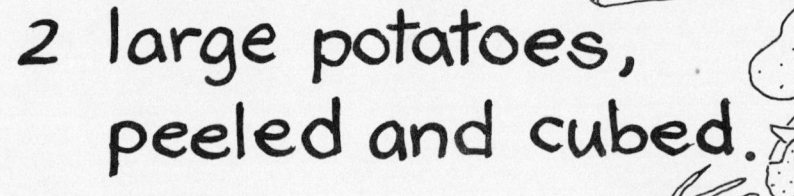

2 large potatoes, peeled and cubed.

½ onion, sliced

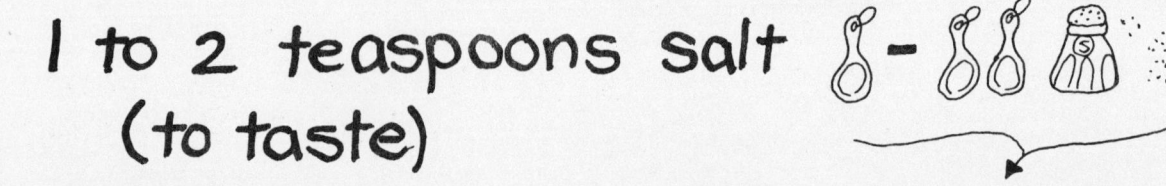

1 to 2 teaspoons salt (to taste)

Put all the ingredients in a large pot half full of water.

Let it boil until potatoes are done – 35 minutes.

Serve hot with Buckskin Bread. (page 73)

145 Isabelle Ides – Basket Maker

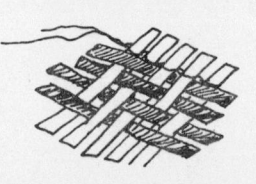

Cooked Play Dough

1 cup flour
1 tablespoon oil
1 cup water
½ cup salt
2 teaspoons cream of tartar
food coloring
tempera paint

Combine all ingredients in a sauce pan.

Cook over medium heat.

Stir constantly until mixture forms a ball.

Knead until smooth.
Store in a covered container.

Playful Peanut Butter Dough

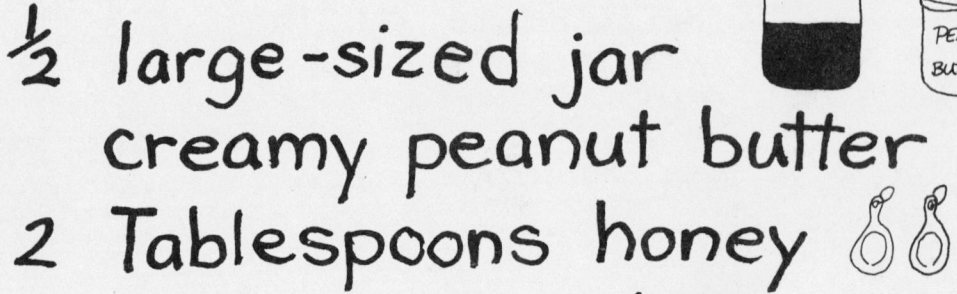

½ large-sized jar creamy peanut butter

2 Tablespoons honey

2 cups powdered milk

raisins

miniature marshmallows

Put peanut butter into a bowl.

Add honey and some of the powdered milk.

Mix it all up with your hands.

Playful Peanut Butter Dough cont'd.

Keep adding powdered milk until the dough feels soft and playful.

Use it like playdough. Mold it into shapes.

Or use cookie cutters.

Make designs using raisins and marshmallows.

Baker's Clay

4 cups flour
1½ cups water
1 cup salt

Mix all ingredients in a bowl.

Knead dough 5 to 10 minutes.

Roll out dough to ¼" thickness.

Cut with decorative cookie cutters. Make hole at top.

Bake at 250° for 2 hours or until hard.

When cool, paint and then spray with clear varnish.

149 Makes great Christmas decorations to hang on trees.

Crunchy Chocolate Fondue

large marshmallows
2 king-sized chocolate crunch candy bars 
1 cup evaporated milk 
bananas 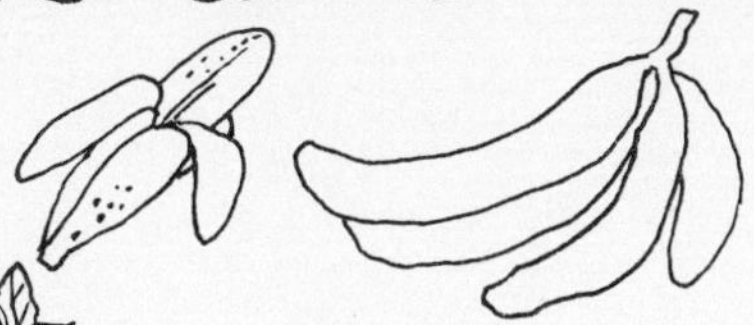
apples 
maraschino cherries with stems

Break candy into pieces.

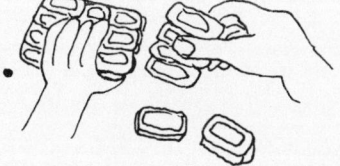

Place candy and milk in fondue pot or heavy sauce pan 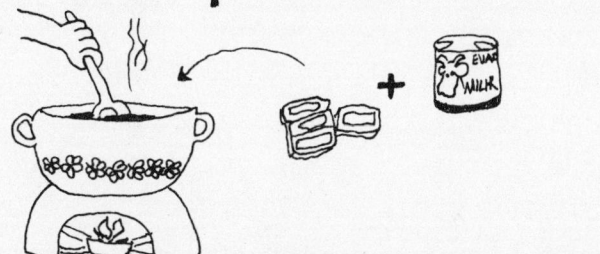  over medium heat, stirring occasionally until chocolate melts.

Chocolate Fondue cont'd.

Slice bananas and apples into bite-sized pieces.

Spear marshmallows, bananas, and apples with fondue forks or toothpicks.

Dip into melted chocolate.

Hold cherries by stems to dip.

Peanut Butter Fondue

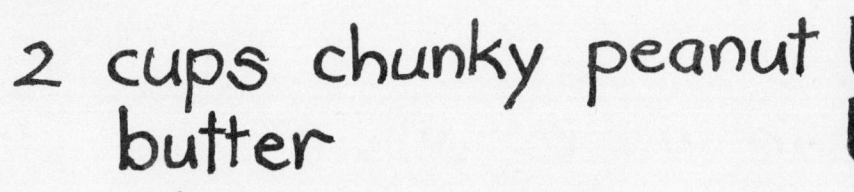

- 2 cups chunky peanut butter 
- 1 5⅓-ounce can evaporated milk 
- 1 cup light brown sugar
- ¼ cup margarine 
- ⅛ teaspoon salt

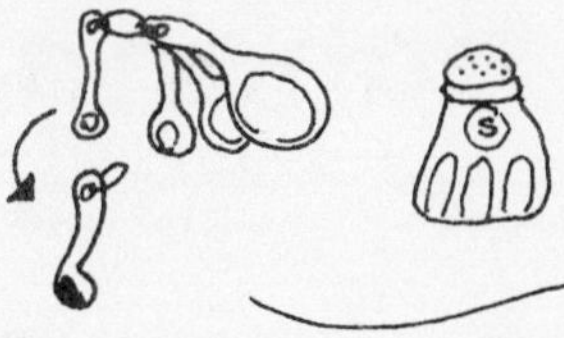

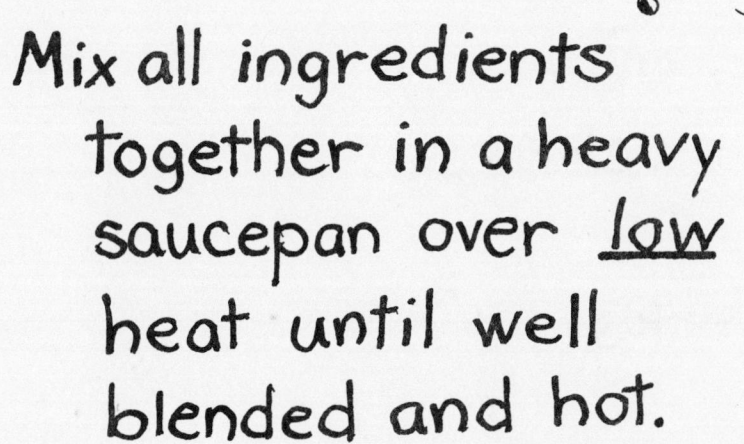

Mix all ingredients together in a heavy saucepan over <u>low</u> heat until well blended and hot.

Stir occasionally.

Peanut Butter Fondue cont'd.

Keep fondue warm while you dunk apple wedges,

marshmallows,

bananas,

and pieces of graham crackers.

Use fondue forks or wooden toothpicks for dunking.

Peanut Butter

1 bag of peanuts in their shells.
peanut oil
salt

Shell the peanuts.

Remove the red skins.

Put peanuts into a blender.

Blend until smooth.

Add a few teaspoons peanut oil if needed.

Serve on crackers.

Butter

2 cups whipping cream
old-fashioned butter churn

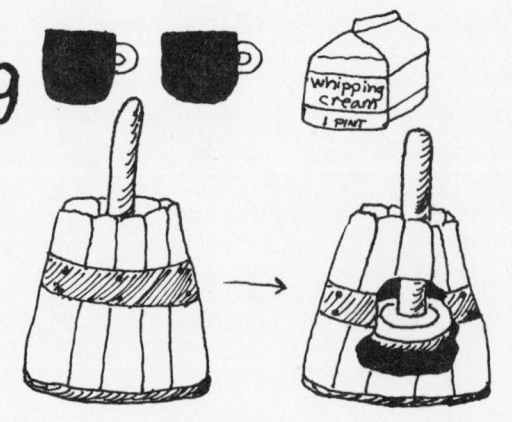

Keep cream in refrigerator until day of use. Take the cream out of refrigerator and let it warm up to room temperature.

Pour cream into churn and take turns turning the handle until butter forms.

Pour off the buttermilk and taste it.

Butter cont'd.

Now taste the unsalted butter
left in the churn.

Next add salt
to the butter
and spread it on crackers.

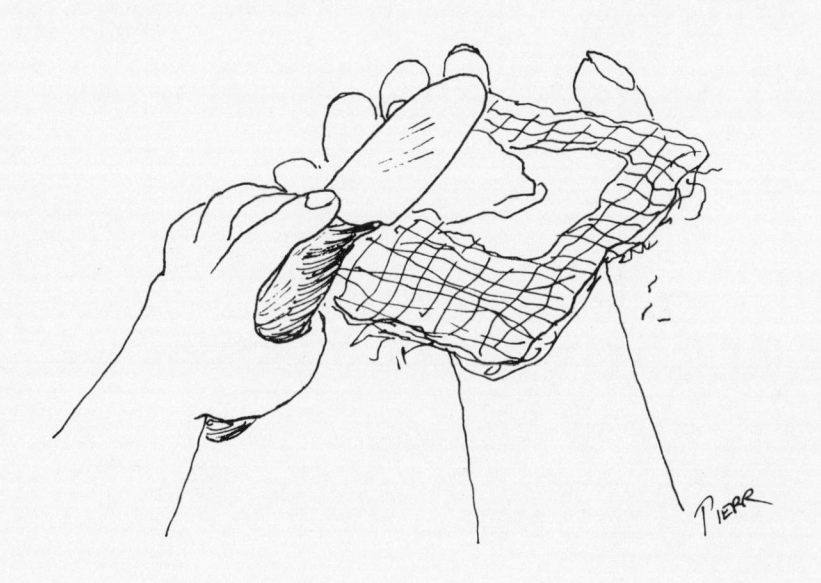

156

Vanilla Ice Cream

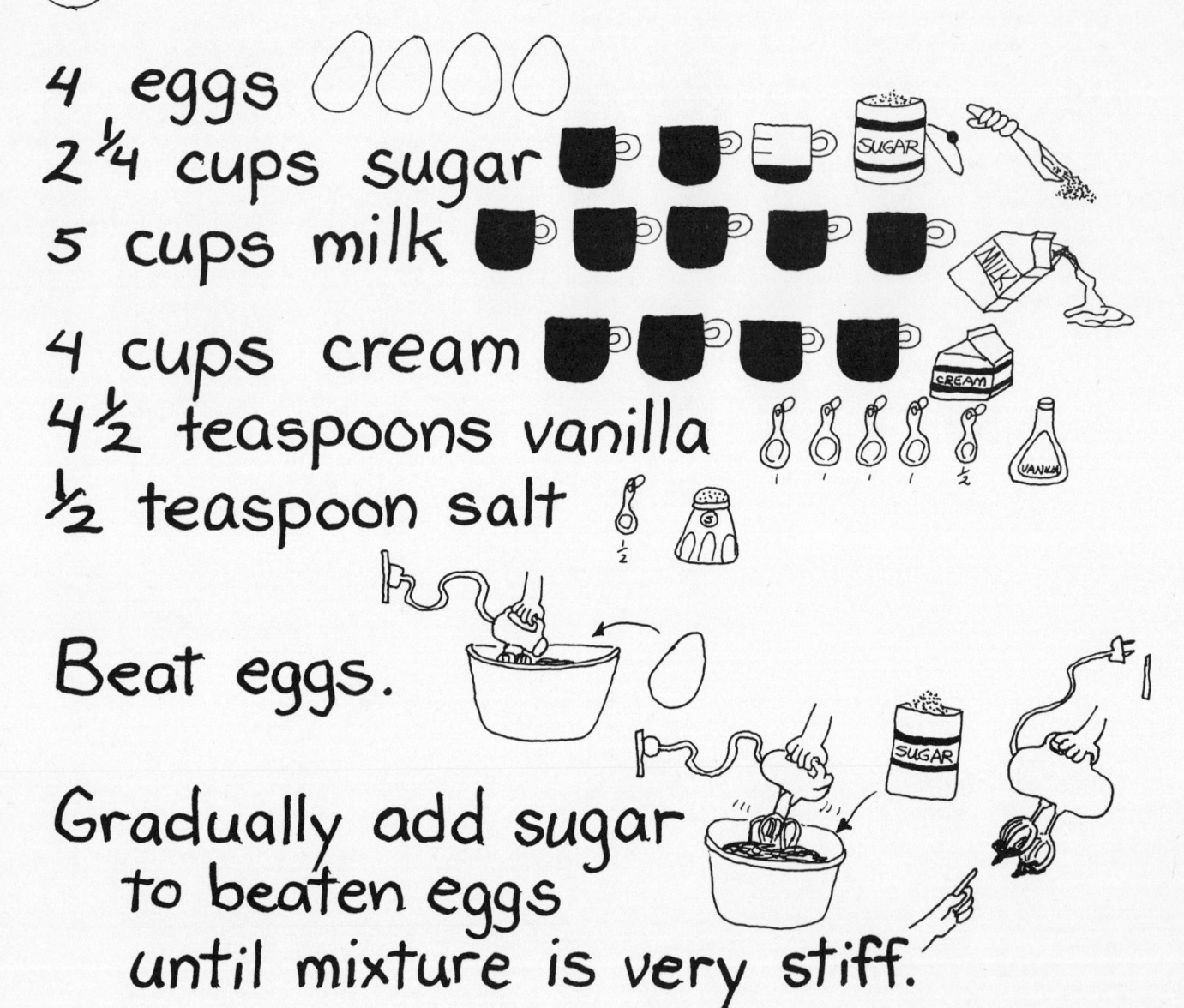

4 eggs
2¼ cups sugar
5 cups milk
4 cups cream
4½ teaspoons vanilla
½ teaspoon salt

Beat eggs.

Gradually add sugar to beaten eggs until mixture is very stiff.

Add remaining ingredients and mix thoroughly.

Vanilla Ice Cream cont'd.

Pour into gallon ice cream freezer.

Layer ice and rock salt in freezer.

Take turns cranking until ice cream is thick.

Blackberry Ice Cream

1 can Eagle Brand milk
1 can evaporated milk
1 cup sugar
1 teaspoon vanilla
3 eggs
2 quarts whole milk

Mix all ingredients together in large bowl.

Pour into ice cream container.

Pack ice and rock salt around the container. (8 to 1 is the proportion of ice to rock salt.)

Blackberry Ice Cream cont'd.

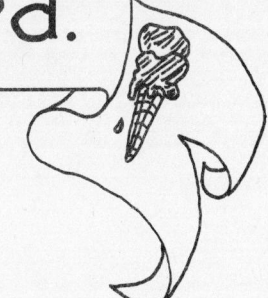

Crank until the mixture thickens.

Then add 1 or 2 cups: ☕ or ☕☕
of fresh blackberries.

Fun With Food

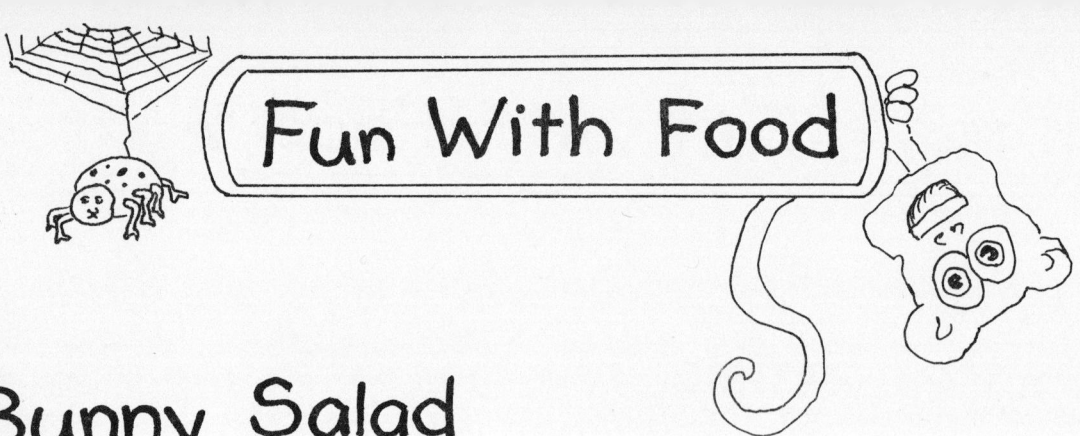

Bunny Salad

Place lettuce leaf on plate.

Place 1 chilled pear half upside down on lettuce leaf.

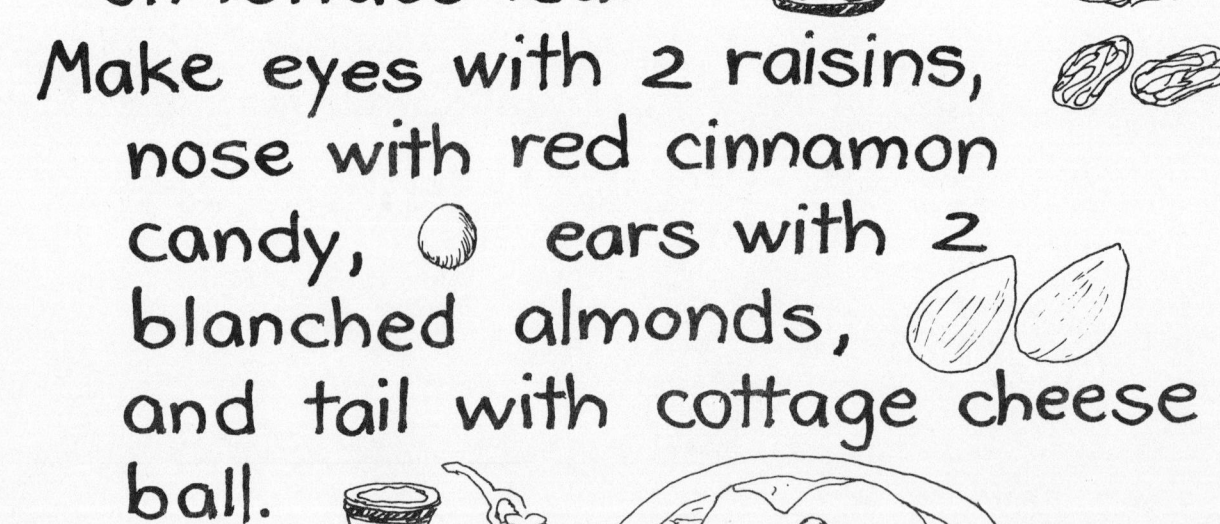

Make eyes with 2 raisins, nose with red cinnamon candy, ears with 2 blanched almonds, and tail with cottage cheese ball.

161

More Fun with Food

Candle Salad

← maraschino cherry
← fastened with toothpick

← half a banana

← pineapple ring

← lettuce leaf

Fruit Tree

Use fresh grapes, cherries, cheese cubes, and cut up pears, apples, or peaches, or drained fruit cocktail.

toothpick
banana →
pineapple ring
← lettuce leaf

162

More and More Fun with Food

Celery Carts

- celery
- carrot slice
- toothpicks

Fill cart with peanut butter or cream cheese mixed with pineapple.

Marshmallow Creatures

large marshmallows
small marshmallows
toothpicks (some
  broken in half)
red hot candies
gumdrops
raisins

More and More and More Fun with Food

Marshmallow Creatures cont'd.

coconut
food coloring (YELLOW, RED, GREEN, BLUE)

Use toothpicks to fasten parts of body together, and use toothpicks dipped in food coloring to draw faces.

Color coconut by shaking it in a quart jar with ½ teaspoon food coloring.

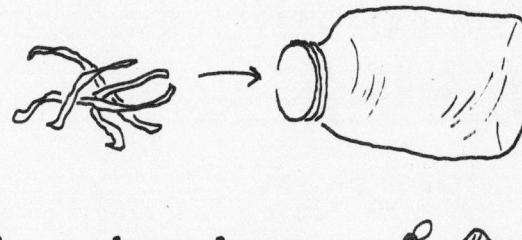

Index

A
African Slush Punch, 125-126
Aggression Cookies, 45
Apple Crisp, 113-114
Apple Salad, 109
Applesauce, 111
Applesauce, Blender, 110
Aunt Nora's Buckskin Bread, 73-74

B
Baker's Clay, 149
Bananas, Things to do with, 121-122
Beverages
    African Slush Punch, 125-126
    Eggnog, 131
    Essie's Supershake, 128
    Fruit Shake, 127
    Hot Cider and Cinnamon Sticks, 130
    Witches' Caldron, 129
Blackberry Ice Cream, 159-160
Blender Applesauce, 110
Breads
    Buckskin Bread, Aunt Nora's, 73-74
    Corn Bread, 70
    Fry Bread, Indian, 75-76
    Gingerbread, 79-80
    Pumpkin Bread, 71-72
    White Bread, 64-67
    Whole Wheat Bread, Honey, 68-69
Butter, 155-156
Butterscotch Crunchies, 3
Butterscotch Flings, 25-26

C
Candies
    Caramel Stickies, 40-41
Cereal Candy, 34
Christmas Present Fudge, 35-36
Chocolate Candies, 37
Creamy Cheese Mints, 44
    Molasses Taffy, 42-43
    S'Mores, 39
    Yummies for Tummies, 38
Caramel Apples, 115-116
Caramel Stickies, 40-41
Carrot-Coconut Salad, 106
Cereal Candy, 34
Chewy Yum Yums, 19
Chicken Soup with Rice, 140-142
Chocolate Candies, 37
Chocolate Yummies, 17-18
Christmas Present Fudge, 35-36
Coconut Pudding, 123-124
Cooked Playdough, 146
Cookies
    Aggression Cookies, 45
    Butterscotch Crunchies, 3
    Chewy Yum Yums, 19
    Chocolate Yummies, 17-18
    Easy Walnut Panocha, 12
    Fa Shang Bo, 16
    Fried Cookies, 4-6
    Fudge Cookies, 7-8
    Gingerbread People, 46-48
    Graham Cracker No-Bake Cookies, 9
    Granola, 55-56
    Macroons, 50
    Metric Peanut Butter Balls, 11
    Molasses Cookies, Grandma's, 57-58
    No Bake Cookies, 10
    Party Sugar Cookies, 59-60
    Peanut Butter Cookies, 51-52
    Peanut Butter Quickies, 49
    Rice Crispies Bars, 15
    Sesame Seed Honey Balls, 13-14
    Sunflower Seed Cookies, 53-54
    Unbaked Peanut Butter Cookies, 2

Index

C
Cooking a Pumpkin, 135
Corn Bread, 70
Corn Flake Balls, 20
Cranberry Relish, 133-134
Creamy Cheese Mints, 44
Creamy Frosting, 63
Creamy Pumpkin Pie Filling, 99-100
Crunchy Chocolate Fondue, 150-151

E
Easy Walnut Panocha, 12
Egg Yolk Paint, 61-62
Essie's Supershake, 128

F
Fa Shang Bo, 16
Finger Jello, 118-119
Fish Stew, Isabelle's, 145
Fondue
    Crunchy Chocolate Fondue, 150-151
    Peanut Butter Fondue, 152-153
French Toast, 86
Fried Cookies, 4-6
Frosting, Creamy, 63
Fruit Jell, 117
Fruit Salad, 105
Fruit Shake, 127
Fudge Cookies, 7-8
Fudge, Christmas Present, 35-36
Fun with Food, 161-164

G
Gingerbread, 79-80
Gingerbread People, 46-48
Graham Cracker Crusts, Individual, 94
Graham Cracker No-Bake Cookies, 9
Grandma's Molasses Cookies, 57-58
Granola, 55-56
Grape Jelly, 132

H
Helen's Popcorn Balls, 30-31
Honeyed Popcorn Balls, 32-33
Honey Whole Wheat Bread, 68-69
Hot Cider with Cinnamon Sticks, 130

I
Ice Cream
    Blackberry Ice Cream, 159-160
    Vanilla Ice Cream, 157-158
Icings
    Creamy Frosting, 63
    Egg Yolk Paint, 61-62
Indian Fry Bread, 75-76
Individual Graham Cracker Crusts, 94
Individual Pizzas, 95-96
Isabelle's Fish Stew, 145

J
Jello
    Finger Jello, 118-119
    Fruit Jell, 117
Jelly, Grape, 132

M
Macroons, 50
Many Muffins Mix, 77-78
Marshmallow Fruit Salad, 103-104
Melon Ball Salad, 101-102
Metric Peanut Balls, 11
Molasses Cheerios Balls, 23-24
Molasses Cookies, Grandma's, 57-58
Molasses Taffy, 42-43

N
No Bake Cookies, 10
No Bake Cookies, Graham Cracker, 9

P
Pancakes
    Potato Pancakes, 85
    Swedish Pancakes, 81-82
    Wheat Pancakes, 83-84

Index

P
Party Sugar Cookies, 59-60
Patting Pie Crust, 98
Peanut Butter, 154
Peanut Butter Balls, Metric, 11
Peanut Butter Cookies, 51-52
Peanut Butter Fondue, 152-153
Peanut Butter Quickies, 49
Peanut Yummies, 21-22
Pie Crust, Patting, 98
Pie Filling, Creamy Pumpkin, 99-100
Pie, Pumpkin, 97
Pizzas, Individual, 95-96
Playdough
    Baker's Clay, 149
    Cooked Playdough, 146
    Playful Peanut Butter Dough, 147-148
Popcorn, 27
Popcorn Balls
    Helen's Popcorn Balls, 30-31
    Honeyed Popcorn Balls, 32-33
Popcorn Cake, 28-29
Potato Pancakes, 85
Pretzels, Soft, 89-90
Prunes, Walnut Stuffed, 120
Pudding, Coconut, 123-124
Pumpkin Bread, 71-72
Pumpkin, Cooking a, 135
Pumpkin Pie, 97
Pumpkin Seeds, Toasted, 136

R
Rice Crispies Bars, 15

S
Salads
    Apple Salad, 109
    Carrot-Coconut Salad, 106
    Fruit Salad, 105
    Marshmallow Fruit Salad, 103-104
    Melon Ball Salad, 101-102
    Tossed Vegetable Salad, 107-108

S
Sesame Seed Honey Balls, 13-14
S'Mores, 39
Soft Pretzels, 89-90
Sopapillas, 91-92
Soups
    Chicken Soup with Rice, 140-142
    Fish Stew, Isabelle's, 145
    Stone Soup, 143-144
Sprouts, 137-139
Stone Soup, 143-144
Sunflower Seed Cookies, 53-54
Swedish Pancakes, 81-82

T
Things to do with Bananas, 121-122
Toasted Pumpkin Seeds, 136
Tortillas, 93
Tossed Vegetable Salad, 107-108

U
Unbaked Peanut Butter Cookies, 2

V
Vanilla Ice Cream, 157-158
Vegetable Salad, Tossed, 107-108

W
Waffles, 87-88
Walnut Stuffed Prunes, 120
Wheat Pancakes, 83-84
White Bread, 64-67
Whole Wheat Bread, Honey, 68-69
Witches' Caldron, 129

Y
Yummies for Tummies, 38